The Murder of Vanessa Guillen

Pete Dove

Published by Trellis Publishing, 2021.

While every precaution has been taken in the preparation of this book, the publisher assumes no responsibility for errors or omissions, or for damages resulting from the use of the information contained herein.

THE MURDER OF VANESSA GUILLEN

First edition. July 13, 2021.

Copyright © 2021 Pete Dove.

ISBN: 979-8224195596

Written by Pete Dove.

THE MURDER OF VANESSA GUILLEN

PETE DOVE

A Betrayal of Trust

'For Immediate Release' is printed near the top, in black, bold capitals. The page is headed 'United States Army', and under this, 'Criminal Investigation Command'. A gold badge, with the emblem of an eagle sitting atop, is emblazoned with a blue circle within which are the words 'CIC Agent'. A media contact number is below.

If a low budget movie were trying to impress a tough teenage audience, the sort where naivety lies just below the surface of acned skin, it is the sort of heading they would produce. Fifteen-year olds, especially marshmallow hardened boys, their top lip bum fluff a badge of honour, love that kind of thing. All bluster and boast.

'Public's Help Sought in Locating Fort Hood Soldier' states the headline proper, each word beginning with a strictly unnecessary capital letter. 'Quantico, VA' begins the content itself, lest any editor thinking of running the story should wonder whether or not the press release is real. Quantico – FBI – 'Silence of the Lambs'. This is serious, everybody. Listen to us.

Two photographs are printed, one shows the smiling face of a vivacious girl, dark of skin and bright of eye. She looks far too young to carry a gun or die for her country. Although that is (in a way) what she has done. The other photo is blurred. It looks like the sort of picture taken in a badly lit passport photo booth. Her eyes are three quarters closed, as though she is under the influence of something unhealthy, although it is just that she is blinking at the flash blinding in her eyes. It is a remarkably insensitive photo, almost certainly of little help to a member of the public asked to look out for the young soldier. Surely, the Criminal Investigation Command could have found a better picture to share with the worried world?

Then, perhaps not. Because the release is dated April 24th, 2020. It has been under forty-eight hours since Vanessa Guillen was reported missing from the Regimental Engineer Squadron HQ located at Fort Hood, Texas. Perhaps, instead of mocking the CIC's reliance on hyperbole – of layout, if not content – we should congratulate them on moving so quickly, of spotting a potential crime and giving the public the best chance of helping out immediately, when their assistance will do most good. Usually, the first twenty-four hours are the most important in finding a person alive when they go missing. If they did not quite make that deadline, the CIC were at least not far behind.

Maybe. The whole press release is, though, overly dramatic. Very Ethan Hunt. Very summer blockbuster movie. Still, they may well have had their reasons for this. Perhaps their psychological profilers had told them, based on limited information and lots of past experience, that this was the form most likely to get results. Sadly, though, it did not in Vanessa's case.

Vanessa Guillen, born on September 30th, 1999 was just twenty years old when she died. She grew up in the south east corner of Houston and attended high school locally. A splendid mural, painted by Alex 'Donkeeboy' Roman Jr., now remembers her in that quarter. It is, appropriately enough, painted onto the wall of a branch of the Mexican food chain, Taqueria Del Sol, in the neighbourhood in which she grew up. Below the wall, flowers, candles and messages are left by people shocked not only by the violent death of one of their own, but by what is emerging from the terrible event. Angels overlook these offerings – real (in their iconic form) as well as metaphorical. As Donkeeboy himself wrote: 'She was serving our country. It takes a lot of courage to be able to do that. We're supposed to respect our soldiers who sacrifice themselves to go out and fight for our country. If we don't respect our soldiers, who are we going to respect? Who's going to respect us?'

The Guillen family is a large one. As well as Vanessa, her parents, Rogelio and Gloria, have five other children. She attended the Cesar E Chavez High School until she graduated in 2018, with a successful academic and sporting record behind her. She passed out in the top fifteen per cent of her class, and played soccer, jogged, loved track athletics and adored swimming. After joining the army, she had trained as a small arms and artillery repairer. At the time of her death, she was ranked as a Private First Class (Pfc), but was posthumously promoted to a Specialist. This means that she would have been paid as a corporal, although would not have shared other benefits of the rank. An unnecessary but welcome gesture? Or grudging recognition by the Army that as an institution it bore some responsibility for her death, and as such the promotion was no more than a piece of mindless tokenism? That is up to us, as individuals, to decide. Certainly, that the US Secretary of the Army, Ryan D. McCarthy, announced on July 1st that a 'full independent review' into Vanessa's death will be launched gives evidence that some of the great institutions of American life are causing embarrassment, or worse. (George Floyd died at the hands, or knee, of a police officer just a month later.)

However, that is not the only political fallout likely to emerge from this case. Texan representative Sylvia Garcia was joined by no less than eighty seven other members of Congress in seeking an independent investigation, to be conducted by the Department of Defense, which would examine the conduct of the search for Vanessa carried out by military officials. She tweeted, on July 6th, 2020, 'Today, 87 of my colleagues joined me in expressing support for...the @DeptofDefense Acting Inspector General to conduct an independent investigation into Fort Hood's handling of SPC Vanessa Guillen's case.'

The Cesar E Chavez High School is located in the Allendale (Meadowbank) area of Houston. It is one of the poorer parts of the city. Here, more than eighty per cent of residents come from Hispanic origins. Educational attainment is often low, with nearly half of all children failing to complete High School, nearly twice the average than for Houston as a whole. A quarter of the population can either only barely speak English or have none of the language at all and there is the suggestion that many of the population there are exploited. With a high percentage of adults renting their homes, the cost of such property is relatively high whilst owner occupiers typically inhabit cheaper properties. Household income is often low, and average size of households is double that, at 5.2 people, of Houston as a whole.

Vanessa Guillen must have believed that, by signing up to life as a soldier, she was taking her opportunity to leave the poverty of the area in which she grew up behind and finding new opportunities in her life.

Instead, what she discovered was the sort of harassment, bullying and danger to which she may well have seen regularly in the Allendale area in which she lived.

So, what happened to induce such a massive panic and urge for justice in the political elite of the United States? If this reaction to the death, as terrible as that is, of one young soldier seems a little extreme, then it becomes apparent that there must be more to Vanessa's death than the gory facts of her murder.

There is. She was last seen on April 22nd, 2020, in the parking lot of her Regimental Engineer Squadron Headquarters (3rd Cavalry Regiment on Fort Hood continued the pedantic press release issued by the base at which she was serving). She was wearing a black T shirt and 'purple fitness-type pants.'

She had left behind her belongings. These included her car keys, wallet and ID card, as well as her barracks room key, which were found in the armory room where she had been working earlier in the day. The last use of her phone was a text she had sent to another soldier working at the base, US Army Specialist Aaron Robinson, also 20, about whom more follows later.

It seems, therefore, that given she had left behind so many important personal belongings, she had seen the visit to the parking lot as likely to be brief, and routine. She had clearly been expecting to return to the armory shortly after completing whatever task she had been required, or wanted, to do.

Vanessa's family had become increasingly concerned on the 22nd April when they failed to get replies to texts sent to her. Her sister, Marya, visited the nearby base, to check on Vanessa's wellbeing Without explanation, she was turned away. Only after a panic-stricken night were the Guillen's told that Vanessa was not on the base and appeared to be missing. The authority's opacity continued for some time, the family's lawyer even accusing officers of 'smirking' behind their secretive approach. They refused to tell the Guillens who had called Vanessa's phone, with whom she was working when she went missing, and what she was doing.

With no sign of the young soccer fan, the Army released the press release reported at the opening of this article. However, little if any in the way of further news was forthcoming over the next couple of months. Until, that is, the report of the discovery of remains on June 30th, more than two months after her disappearance.

Information received had led investigators to an area close to the Leon River. This was about thirty miles, and an hour's drive, away from the Fort Hood Army base. A thirty-mile radius from any centre covers an enormous area. Clearly, whatever lead investigators received, it was a good one. Later, agents who worked for the US Army's Criminal Investigation Command returned to the scene, in Bell County, Texas, and there human remains were discovered. The Army's CID issued a statement shortly after this.

'Due to extensive investigative work conducted by Special Agents from the US Army Criminal Investigation Command,' they stated, with more than a nod to their own detective prowess, 'agents have discovered what has been described as partial human remains after an analysis from a forensic anthropologist. Army CID agents are currently on scene with the Texas Rangers, the FBI and Bell County Sheriff's Department.'

Whilst in that particular announcement, the Army was keen to emphasise that no identification had yet been made for the remains, there was little reading between the lines required to realise that that they belonged to missing Vanessa. However, Tim Miller, who set up and runs the charity Texas EquuSearch, was very clear. 'The search for Vanessa is now over,' he told media channels.

EquuSearch specialises in seeking out missing people. Apparently, during their first search in the area, investigators had discovered evidence located in the Leon River itself. On their return, they had discovered a shallow grave, with the remains inside.

'It's believed to be her,' continued Miller, 'pending positive identification which that will have to be determined by the medical examiner's office, but I'm confident to say the search for Vanessa is now over.'

In their typically, opaque, secretive way, Army investigators made it clear that the public would have to be satisfied with that news. 'Due to the ongoing criminal investigation, no further information will be released at this time,' they stated. Sensible protection of their investigation? Or the beginnings of a cover up? Difficult to say, although the members of Congress who pressed for an independent review of the investigation just a week later must clearly have had doubts about the direction in which the investigation was heading. It was the weekend of 4th July that confirmation was provided for certain, backing up Tim Miller's assertions, that the remains were those of Vanessa.

With painful irony, the call which ended all hope for the Guillen family that Vanessa might still be alive arrived on the birthday of sister Marya. It was the worst present she could possibly receive, made even more horrendous by the fact that it was she who took the call.

'There's not much that can explain what we're feeling,' said Marya. 'I feel an empty presence in my chest. And for my mom, it's hard to accept. But she knows that heaven has an angel.' Vanessa was especially close to Marya. It was she who flew out to attend the ceremony when

Vanessa finished training, and the two together would apply each other's make up, or choose outfits for dates and parties.

It is by examining the actions of Vanessa's family, over those painful weeks when the Army was keeping matters as close to its vast chest as it could, that we can begin to see just why Congress is demanding action.

Despite her commitment to her schooling and learning, Vanessa always had a goal to serve in the military, right from the days as a small child when she would play soldiers with her brother's toy guns and tell her mother that one day she would defend her country. Gloria was wary of such an ambition, but it did not go away, and Vanessa enlisted when she was just 18, not telling her mother until she had signed the paperwork lest she should be dissuaded from her ambition. The harsh reality of her daughter's murder has made Gloria reflect painfully on that moment. 'It made me cry so much that day, all day I cried...I said, "Don't sign, don't sign,' she recalled. 'My mother's intuition warned me of the pain I was going to feel.'

Rogelio, too, feels the suffering of a parent. On the day Vanessa disappeared, he recalls a strange and sudden discomfort. 'After lunch, after 12p.m, I felt a strong pain in my chest. Never in my life have I felt something like that,' he said.

Vanessa died by being bludgeoned to death with a hammer. Violent, appalling, but, as a manner of death, in little doubt. It is what lay behind the attack, it seems, that makes this case so special. Because in their frequent trips between their home in Texas and Washington, the Guillen family were chipping away at the wall successive Governments, including the present incumbents, have put up to hide one of the last taboos of American society. That its mighty, untouchable, immense and respected armed forces might be a hotbed for sexual harassment, sexual bullying and sexual assault.

'If you can't trust the army, who can you trust?' as a certain Houston based mural artist might have said.

As the story gradually broke, cutting through the wall of silence the Army was trying to impose, others began to take up the call. Celebrities, lawmakers, artists. Even, a very brave Presidential candidate. Such a stance is admirable indeed for a person with high political ambitions. Especially so, many will argue, in Trump's America of popularism and intolerance of youth. Doubly so when the victim is Hispanic. It might be said. Not by all. But by enough.

Vanessa had, prior to her death, reported to her family that she had fallen victim of a predator within the army. And she did not know what to do about it. Her family remain determined to bring about change in the way the military deals with reports of sexual assault and harassment. For too long, it has been the secret which does not speak its name.

Meanwhile, though, officials at Fort Hood were trying to spin out the usual mix of surprised outrage and platitudes. They would complete their own investigation into the claims that soldiers were sexually harassed at their base, including, of course, soon to be Specialist Guillen. They would review their own policies and responses to such claims and allegations and ensure that any shortcomings in such procedures are addressed. At the same time, Colonel Ralph Overland, commander of the 3rd Cavalry Regiment located at the base, told reporters that thousands of soldiers had taken part in the search for Vanessa's body. 'We never quit,' he said, 'and we never leave a fallen comrade.'

Many believe that Vanessa, and others like her, had already been abandoned, and for too long. She had been abandoned by an institution which, like so many others, saw the sexual harassment and assault of young, vulnerable soldiers – usually (but not always) female - as a price to bear. And also, a secret, one to keep tightly locked behind its own closed doors.

When Marya had received the call telling her that her sister was dead, she had wanted to wait until her family returned home from their latest trip before telling them. But her mother, Gloria, 42, had, with a parent's instinct, known something was wrong, and had needed medical treatment for a panic attack close to the time that the news was being received by Marya.

'It's horrible,' said Gloria, speaking in her native Spanish. 'It's maddening. As her mother, I cannot sleep.' In the immediate aftermath of the terrible news, the family have relied on their community, their priest and their Catholic faith for whatever comfort they can provide.

A small part of that comfort, conversely, is that at least the agony of waiting and not knowing is past. 'I do feel that' said Marya, 'at this point, it was kind of like God's gift to me that we were able to find her despite the circumstances. People can go missing for years, and having no answers is much worse than having an answer.'

Vanessa's younger sister, Lupe, also spoke out about the horror of what her sibling had been through. 'My sister's a human being,' she said, tears rendering her voice hard to follow. 'I want justice, and I want answers.' Later, she gave an insight into the suffering she, and her family, were experiencing. 'The last 75 days for me, for my family – I haven't slept. It has been a nightmare,' she said.

Now Marya is spearheading the family's campaign for that justice, and to make sure that no other soldiers suffer as her sister did in the future. As the eldest of the six siblings, she felt that she must take responsibility for seeking the change surely the whole of America wants. A change so that victims of sexual harassment and assault who are working in the armed forces have somewhere to turn to. 'I just hope none of this is in vain,' she said.

The concerns are justified. Recent military history is littered with stories of soldiers suffering not only as the result of predatory behaviour from their colleagues, but also when they try to make such attacks known. As Lupe said, it is the publicity surrounding Vanessa's death, which, thanks to the actions of her family and politicians such as Democratic Presidential Candidate Joe Biden Jr, has captured the attention of the press. It has done so despite attempts from the authorities to close access to such information. In turn, that has encouraged hundreds of other victims to come forward.

Maybe, now they will not see their claims dismissed or, as Vanessa was sure would happen if she reported the attacks on her, disbelieved. That is something younger sister Lupe is determined that the family will address now. 'We're going to be my sister's voice,' she said. 'She's going to be heard, and she's going to be remembered.'

Perhaps even the army itself is taking note. 'We are saddened and deeply troubled by the loss of one of our own, Spc Vanessa Guillen,' it said in a recent statement. It went on to add that the Army was 'committed to finding justice for Vanessa and her family.' That justice will, of course need to have two elements. Firstly, and perhaps more easily, identification of the person who killed Vanessa. The second challenge is undoubtedly more difficult, for an institution so large and hard to turn as a tradition-filled one such as the army. That is to recognise that it was its own practices, traditions and procedures which encouraged and allowed the sort of sexual harassment and bullying – often worse – from which Vanessa suffered, and so many continue to endure today.

In Vanessa's case, it seems as though the harassment came from a more senior officer. She reported to her family that a sergeant was hassling her. 'I haven't reported him,' she told her mother, 'because they won't believe me. They laugh at all the girls that have gone and they don't believe them.' The army, it seems, believed itself immune from the #MeToo outrages.

Change involves recognising, and redressing, the many careers that have been ruined, lives that have been spoiled by the US Army's failure to recognise that the victims of sexual attacks are not partly (and sometimes, it seems, accused of being mostly) guilty of the crime to which they have fallen victim. Such attitudes in military institutions are not limited to the US. In Britain, the scandal over bullying at one particular barracks, Deep Cut, continues to roll on; here several young soldiers committed suicide, the victims of bullying of the institutional variety as well as the errant behaviour of one or two individuals. In Britain, the army has largely failed to face up to its responsibilities towards these victims, although some changes have resulted. It is hoped that the US army can accept more responsibility, understand that it needs to change, quickly and drastically, if further tragedies such as the one which befell Vanessa are to cease. Let us hope it will do so. That, unlike the press release highlighted at the beginning of this piece, the institution will show a more mature approach to its duty and stop acting like it lives in the action thrilled fantasy world of fifteen-year-old boys. James Bond is fiction, not truth.

The day after Vanessa's remains were found, Aaron Robinson disappeared. Later, his body was found, and it appeared as though he had shot himself. To many, his suicide satisfies at least half the case, putting to bed doubts about who killed Vanessa. His girlfriend, who is facing charges which allege she helped him to dispose of Vanessa's body, told investigators that her boyfriend had struck a female soldier in the head with a hammer multiple times...'killing her on Fort Hood.' She went on to say that Robinson then 'placed his victim in a box.'

The strong possibility exists, therefore, that Robinson did kill Vanessa, although her harasser was a Sergeant, not a Specialist like Robinson. However, the army has been secretive throughout and Robinson is now dead, which means he cannot defend himself. These facts, too, have raised suspicions in some quarters. Aaron Robinson probably did kill his colleague, and he probably shot himself when filled with fear of discovery, remorse and guilt. But he also makes for a convenient scapegoat. Whether the truth will ever come out, we cannot say. Given precedents, it seems unlikely.

Whilst nobody can be said to be guilty until it is proved so, at the time of writing at least it seems as though this may be an open and shut matter. Tragic, terrible, but nevertheless soon to be closed. However, this is not the case. The question now is as to whether Vanessa's death is part of a wider concern threatening to embrace the US Army depot in Fort Worth. Or even, the US Army as a whole.

The death of a young woman cannot be mitigated. When that death comes as a result of murder, which seems to be as close to a certainty here as an untried case can be, the loss becomes even more tragic. The fear, the horror which must face the young victim in her final moments are ones about which it is painful to think. If it is hard for us, mere members of the public, imagine, then, what it must be like for her friends. Her family. Her parents.

But this death is not of a random member of the public. Vanessa Guillen had decided to sign up to defend her country. As Steve Campion, of the Houston based news group ABC13 put it in a tweet, 'She is everyone's daughter.' As a member of the armed forces, it was accepted, with heartfelt thanks for her courage, that there could be a time when her life might be in danger. That is the price to be paid for taking the brave decision to protect one's nation. What nobody – the public, her friends, her family, Vanessa herself – should expect is that the biggest danger should come from within one of America's own Army bases. That is not acceptable. It is a betrayal of trust A matter which must be addressed.

Further, that it seems almost certain that Vanessa was the victim of a campaign of sexual harassment from within the Army barracks itself, and that bullying – sexual and otherwise – was one small part of a much more widespread cancer eroding the defensive wall protecting the nation. But by bringing that canker out in the open, Vanessa has done the nation, the personnel of the armed forces and even the institution itself an enormous service.

The press release issued by the CIC back in April 2020 was almost childish in its macho melodrama. But the aftermath of Vanessa's death has made America wake up and open its eyes to reality. Maybe, too, the Army will follow. It will stop pretending it is immune from the standards of decency expected in the remainder of society, it will realise that within its ranks evil exists, and that evil must be made transparent, rooted out and eviscerated. Not hidden behind a veil of pretence. Maybe, the army will grow up. Perhaps, as her family's lawyer, Natalie Khawam hopes, 'Vanessa's Bill' will pass into law, and an independent agency working outside of the military hierarchy's control will be established, an agency to which victims of assault and harassment can report their fears without the risk of the blame for their victimhood falling on themselves.

If so, in no small part that will be down to Vanessa Guillen. The country is proud of her.

MURDER IN TEXAS : THE TRUE STORY OF RHONDA JOHNSON & SHARON SHAW

JAMIE FOSTER

Rhonda Johnson and Sharon Shaw were two teenage girls murdered in 1971. But despite having had their lives taken so long ago, their case is still not satisfactorily solved. It's a story that involves not just two girls being murdered so young, but a potentially innocent man imprisoned for over twenty years, a corrupt police force, a serial killer, and perhaps the wider context of the Texas Killing Fields murders.

The story of the twists and turns involved in finding justice for the two girls continues on until today. Michael Lloyd Self, the man who some believe to have been wrongly imprisoned for the murder of the two girls, has since died in prison of cancer. Because of his passing, and the difficulty that investigators have found in unearthing new evidence, it seemed unlikely that the full story will ever come out.

But not long ago, a revelation and a startling confession have brought Johnson and Shaw's murders back into the limelight. Perhaps, at last, their families can discover the truth of their real killers.

Who were Rhonda Renee Johnson and Sharon Shaw?

Sharon Lynn Shaw was born in Mobile, Alabama to Hoyt Shaw and Mary Ann Collins on August 11th, 1957. Rhonda was born in Houston, Texas to Charles Johnson Sr. and Betty Huey on December 16th, 1956. Not much is known of their early lives, although by 1971 they were living next to one another in Webster, Texas, and were good friends.

Both girls had finished with school for the year and were enjoying their time off together. The day of their disappearance began like many others that summer, with a day out on a pleasant morning. It was August 4th, 1971 and Johnson and Shaw wanted to take a day trip to Galveston, to Wix Ski School, and to visit Doug's Surf and Dive Shop which was nearby. The area also had a Dairy Queen and a popular swimming school, making it very popular with the teenagers of the surrounding area. Given that it was summer, the girls would most likely have preferred to stay all day, but had promised their parents that they would be home by 1pm.

They hitched a ride with a family friend, who took them on the 30 mile journey to Galveston. Unfortunately for the girls' parents, that morning would be the last that they would ever see of their children.

The afternoon came and went, and the girls didn't call home to explain their absence. After they missed dinner that night, their parents began to call their friends to see if they'd heard from them, and called the neighbor who had given them a ride. None of their friends had heard a thing, and the last their neighbor had seen was when the girls had been dropped off at the skiing school and surf club. The girls were soon reported missing by their parents, who went in person to the local police department.

According to Raymond Wix, the owner of Wix Ski School, the girls didn't stay long there that day. In conversation with the Webster Police Department, he had told them that they had headed off after being told that the ski boats weren't running that day due to choppy waters. That was the last that we can say with certainty about the girls' day.

It was in August that the pair crossed paths with the man who would end their lives, but it wasn't until the beginning of 1972 that the girls' bodies were found. Just after the New Year, two young men went fishing near Webster, Texas, their hometown. They came across a skull floating in the marsh, and one of the men wrapped it up in a towel, stowed it away and took it home. After sharing their find with the Harris County Sherriff, the skull was eventually identified as belonging to the missing Rhonda Johnson.

This triggered a large scale search of Taylor Lake and the Bayou, which despite its size took until February 17th to find any more evidence. That day, another skull was found in a nearby drainage ditch, and soon more bones were found. They were identified as belonging to both girls.

Michael Lloyd Self tried and convicted

While the girls' bodies were discovered in early January, it was only in late May the same year that progress began on their case. The city council hired a new police chief that month, Don Morris, who brought with him a new assistant chief, Tommy Deal. Eager that they be seen to be doing something on such a large crime for a small town, the pair acted on a tip they'd received about local man Michael Lloyd Self.

Self was, admittedly, a sex offender known locally who had already been arrested multiple times in 'Peeping Tom' incidents. It was Morris and Deal themselves who visited Self at his place of work, a gas station, where Self was working night shifts at the time. They questioned him on the topic of the 'two girls'- the officers, of course, referring to Johnson and Shaw. Self, however, believed them to mean his estranged wife and new girlfriend, and having been confused went to the police station later that day to clear the matter.

Upon his arrival, he was again questioned about Johnson and Shaw, this time being shown their photographs and interrogated on his connection to them. Self admitted to recognising them, and unfortunately for him, that seemed to be enough evidence for the new chief: he was arrested then and there on the charge of their murders.

Since he was now officially detained at the station- he had, after all, only arrived voluntarily that morning- Self's interrogation could now begin in earnest. Morris and Deal claimed that their suspicions rested on evidence that they had obtained, and urged him to confess. According to Jerry Mitchell, another officer at the police station that day, Self appeared calm and rational throughout the early stages of his questioning, clearly expecting any second that the officers would realise they had the wrong man.

He continued to deny the crimes as the morning wore on, but according to Self, the interrogations became continually more threatening and violent. Morris held him up against the wall, jabbed him with his nightstick, and even threatened to shoot him were he to carry on denying the crimes. Finally, Self had had enough: he wrote out his confession. He would later claim that Morris told him what to write, even forcing him to rewrite his confession several times over, a claim echoed once more by Jerry Mitchell.

During his time in court, Michael claimed that his confession had been forced out of him by the two officers interrogating him. These concerns were quickly dismissed, since after all, which murderer doesn't deny the charges against them?

Self's Confession: Details and Inconsistencies

It is easy to see why a jury or a prosecutor might be taken in by the confession, were they to consider the case 'open and shut' and not give it enough thought. It is particularly detailed with regards to the murders. Self first describes how he picked up Rhonda as he saw her walking along the road, turning around to pick her up in his car. They then drove to the Nassau Bay Yacht Club, where Rhonda found her friend Sharon. He claimed that he provided them with beer, offered them marijuana which they declined, and drove around the Clear Lake area 'feel[ing] good and getting loud.'

As the night wore on, Self's version of events is that Sharon had been hanging out of the window 'hollering at everybody and shooting peace signs at them' as he drove. Since neither of the girls wanted to go home, he claimed they went down to Clear Lake where he tried to assault Rhonda, which she rejected. Since Sharon was out of the car, Self continued assaulting her, and at her continued protests he became angry and hit both Sharon and Rhonda over the head with a Coke bottle repeatedly until they were both unconscious.

He goes on to describe how he drove the girls to an abandoned, dead end road, stripped them of their clothes and dumped their bodies in the Bayou.

Reading back the confession that Self may or may not have been forced to write, it is at least easy to spot several glaring, obvious mistakes. Perhaps the worst is that according to his confession, Self disposed of the girls' bodies more than twenty miles from where they were actually found. Both of the girls were found with their clothes on, not stripped as Self had claimed. Even the method by which he confessed to having murdered Johnson and Shaw was incorrect according to the coroner's report, with Self claiming to have strangled the girls, but their bodies showing no such marks.

Moreover, Sharon's family dispute the confession since it mentions Self picking up the young girl from her family home, which they deny. The confession also states that Self and the two girls were in Webster at 9pm, whereas eyewitnesses disagree and place the two girls- alone- in Galveston instead. The written confession is even further discredited by Self's later verbal confessions, which contradict several key points. For instance, Self repeated his claim during a polygraph test taken three days after his initial arrest that he stripped the girls before dumping their bodies, when they were in fact found with their clothes on.

The story only continues to get stranger. Two weeks after Self was first arrested, while the officers were still building the case against him, he was actually taken from jail by two deputies. They had told Self that they were going to buy him dinner. In fact, they took him out of town to the locations which Self had mentioned in his confessions to take pictures of him as a sort of third and final confession. These photos were even presented in court as evidence.

This episode is mentioned in the court records of Self's appeal. There, the scene is painted as Self agreeing to show the two deputies the various locations involved in the murder. First, the group went to the Sizzler Steak House, where Self said he picked up Rhonda (contradicting his claim that he had picked her up on El Camino Real, a nearby street, where she had been walking). According to this testimony, after picking up Sharon they then went to a Jack in the Box restaurant. The fact that this confession had been so different to his previous one, however, did not constitute enough of a problem for either confession to be inadmissible according to the court records of Self's appeal case.

Time passes by

After Self's conviction, justice did appear to have been done. Trust in the police was higher than it is today; if a man had been arrested, tried, and convicted of a crime then the case was, quite simply, closed. Self, for his part, never gave in. He continually appealed the case and applied for parole, beginning taking the case to an appeals court just a year after his first imprisonment.

According to the court records, Self complained on several grounds. First, he claimed that the evidence presented at his first trial was 'insufficient to sustain his conviction', mostly due to his claim that his confession was forced, but also because the photos taken at the various locations relevant to the case shouldn't have been admitted as evidence.

Unfortunately, each time Self applied for parole, or put his case up for appeal, he was unsuccessful. In the eyes of the law there was little reason to overturn the ruling. Self's first confession did contain some errors, but was also correct on several points, particularly that the bodies were disposed of and found in water. At appeal, the judge decided that enough of the confession corroborated with material evidence to uphold the previous verdict.

While Self's protests had been dismissed, the case still seemed to some to be too flimsy to have justified the certainty of a seventy year sentence. Like many similar cases before his, Self's case was eventually dramatized as part of the TV show, Unresolved Mysteries. David Coburn, a local investigator interviewed in the episode, actually backed up Self's story of Morris' mistreatment of him during his interrogation. Coburn claimed that he had seen Morris' brutality first hand during another interrogation the year before. The show raised the same questions as Self had done, but of course left it to the viewer to decide as to whether he truly was guilty or not.

Morris and Deal's Motives: The Texas Killing Fields

The show also raised the question of why, exactly, Morris and Deal had been so eager to arrest Self on such little evidence. In all of their efforts to extract repeated confessions from the defendant, it certainly seemed that they must have had their reasons. First, Self was well known locally for his sexual misdemeanors. For the city, it would make their lives a lot easier to finally put Self away for a longer sentence. It also made sense for the new chief to make it obvious that he was hard on crime. A new chief not addressing one of the largest and most shocking cases in Webster history would certainly give a bad first impression.

Last, but certainly not least, is the fact that the area had seen an unnaturally large number of murders from the start of the 1970s, which we today call the Texas Killing Fields murders. If Johnson and Shaw really were victims of the same serial killer as the other murders in the area, they were some of the very first to be killed. However, by the time they were discovered, five other girls' bodies had been found in the local area.

Whether law enforcement at the time would have recognised that these murders were perhaps the work of a repeat killer, they would at least have been aware of the spate of local killings, and been desperate to pin the crime on somebody. This, perhaps, was part of the reason why Morris and Deal were more eager than they should have been to try to pin those crimes on Self. At the very least, newspaper clippings from the time of the investigation reveal the public concern over previous missing persons' cases, as well as the deaths of many other young girls from the area. In a copy of The Odessa American from June 10th 1970, the author reveals that Self was suspected to perhaps have had a hand in the many other recent local murders.

The two girls were far from the last victims, however, as the Texas Killing Fields murders continued through the 1980s and 1990s, some even coming after the turn of the century. Almost every victim has been between the ages of 12 and 17, and every victim has been a young girl or woman. In total, at least 30 bodies have been found all within a 25 acre area just off I-45. Even aside from the discovered bodies, many more local girls have gone missing and are featured on websites like The Charley Project, a site dedicated to tracking down missing persons. All of this has led some to believe that the murders must be the work of a serial killer.

They certainly fit the bill: all around the same area, the vast majority of the victims fitting the same description, and a relatively steady pace of killings through the years all suggest the work of one lone actor. The only real argument against the idea is the fact that the killer must somehow have remained at large for so long, despite leaving such an obvious trail. If the murder of Johnson and Shaw really were part of the Texas Killing Fields murders- and given that the murders were often of pairs of young girls around their age, it would seem very likely- then Self could not have been their killer, since the murders continued for long after he was incarcerated.

A Twist in the Tale

Whether the Texas Killing Fields murders were the acts of a lone serial killer, or how he must be innocent if Johnson and Shaw were two victims of that same killer, was irrelevant to Michael Lloyd Self. Despite all of his protestations, appeals, and parole hearings, he remained in prison. It was only in 1998 that any development in this seemingly long-dead case came about. Edward Harold Bell was already in prison, after a manhunt that spanned the globe. He had been on the run since 1978, after the attempted assault of a group of children and the murder of a Marine, Larry Dickens, who had attempted to intervene.

The murder was especially brutal. It had taken place in a normal, suburban street; Bell had been coasting around in his car, searching for girls. Finding a group of young teenagers, he had stopped his car and jumped out, not wearing anything below the waist. Dickens, a local resident, noticed what was happening and attempted to intervene. Unfortunately for him, Dickens didn't like being interrupted.

He went back to his car, picked up a pistol and began shooting. Larry struggled back to the garage, where his mother had been watching the scene, and collapsed in her arms. Bell didn't stop shooting. When he ran out of bullets in his pistol, he went back to his truck to exchange it for his rifle, and carried on.

Bell would have been guaranteed life in prison for the brutal murder, but skipped bail and went on the run for 15 years. In 1984 he be was identified as part of a failed burglary in Texas, but still managed to avoid the police before finally being tracked down in Panama in 1993. Upon his eventual capture, he was finally convicted of the murder of Dickens and received 70 years in prison. Bell's murder of Dickens, too, was featured on Unresolved Mysteries; curiously, Matthew McConaughey caught his first big break on TV playing the role of Larry.

His connection to the Johnson and Shaw case was completely unknown before he confessed not just to their murders, but to the murder of eleven girls in total in the 1970s. The frankly disturbing letters were sent to prosecutors for both Harris County and Galveston County way back in 1998, but were kept under wraps until 2011. The letters initially claimed a tally of seven lives, but in interviews with the Houston Chronicle after their publication admitted to the total of eleven murders. In them, he claimed to have been a part of a government brainwashing program that forced him to assault, rape, and kill young girls.

Who Was Edward Harold Bell?

According to the Houston Chronicle, Bell had a 'normal' early life, 'even exemplary'. A boy scout who went on to earn a degree from Texas A&M, he made his living first as a licensed diver- where he met his wife- before settling as a travelling pharmaceutical salesman in West Texas. On the surface, he seemed like a normal man, with a normal job, and a happy wife and family.

According to Bell himself, however, his childhood was not idyllic. His family were always on the move since his father worked as a gauger at small oil fields across Texas, earning plenty of money to provide for his wife and son but forcing them to live an itinerant lifestyle. Not just this, but Bell also claimed that his father was excessively violent towards his family: in Bell's own words, 'My father thought if he beat you real bad, it would send chemicals into your bloodstream.' Bell fathered three children of his own over the years- but what his family didn't know was that he was leading a sordid double life.

Bell's crimes began much the same way as Self's had done: Bell progressed from peeping tom incidents, to masturbating in public and exposing himself to girls around Texas. According to the Chronicle, he was apprehended committing public indecencies at least twelve times, from Lubbock to Houston; his targets, teenage girls, often in pairs, but always unaccompanied by adults. More often than not, he managed to avoid prosecution or arrest for his actions. He began- at least, he was first caught- in 1968, exposing himself to teenage girls in the town of Sudan. Police and court records show that he continued on and off until at least 1978, the year he murdered Larry Dickens for interrupting an episode of his flashing.

Bell was in and out of mental institutions for a large part of that decade, on referral from court. He somehow didn't receive a single jail sentence for any of his sexual crimes, something which most likely wouldn't happen today. If he had been appropriately dealt with by the police for his previous crimes, the life of Larry Dickens could have been saved. In fairness to the police, however, his violent outburst was entirely unprecedented.

What Happened Next?

It would seem that at last, justice could have been done. Through all the years, Self had maintained his innocence, continued to claim that his confession had been forced, and that despite knowing the girls he had not been involved in their murders. Bell was a known murderer, already in prison, and provided remarkably accurate details with relevance to several missing persons cases in his letters. It would seem that given this detail, and Bell's prior crimes, that his confessions would force prosecutors to re-open the case and for Self's version of events, perhaps, to be reheard and finally believed.

All of this was not to be. As is so often the case with decades-old missing persons cases- in particular cases that seemed as closed as this- the new evidence wasn't treated with the interest it should have been. Astonishingly, Galveston County refused to present the letters to a jury for their consideration, and even worse, Harris County actually lost the letters altogether. Self remained in prison, unaware that a confession had even been made.

One of the prosecutors for Galveston County stated to the Houston Chronicle that he "...didn't believe we had sufficient evidence that we could proceed to grand jury with, and without getting into specifics, that's the decision that had to be made, no matter the temptations to proceed otherwise ... It wasn't for a lack of effort." In fairness to the prosecutors, the evidence to reopen a case of murder- particularly one that already, in the eyes of the law, has been settled- has to be very compelling, and perhaps the confession of a man known to be mentally unstable is not enough. After all, serial killers have been known to confess to crimes they may not have committed to gain infamy, or recapture the spotlight long after their conviction.

It was only two years later that Michael Lloyd Self died in prison, of cancer. If he really was innocent- and on the balance of probabilities, it seems that he may have been- then he will never see justice for his unlawful incarceration, which lasted a total twenty seven years before his death.

As for Bell, he remains in prison. He received 70 years for the inexplicably brutal murder of Larry Dickens, and so any sentence received for the murders of Johnson and Shaw- not to mention the other girls he claimed to have killed in the same letters- would be irrelevant. Bell was in his late 70s at the time of writing, and will die in prison.

The Johnson and Shaw cases are still, officially, the crimes of Michael Lloyd Self, and the case remains closed. Since Bell's letters were received by county prosecutors, no new evidence has come to light; the letters and accompanying information were not considered enough to reopen the case then, and aren't considered enough now. And due to Bell's refusal to co-operate with police, it seems unlikely that any new information on his potential part in the murders will ever be revealed.

BONUS STORY :

Texarkana has always been an unusual place. On the east, you have Texarkana, Arkansas, a small town by any other measurement, yet home to the largest population in Miller County. To the west lies Texarkana, Texas, located in rural Bowie County and lucky enough to have its very own Wal-Mart. Together these twin cities make up what is simply referred to as "Texarkana."

Texarkana is a dusty town, built on a foundation of competing railroads and a Mexican border dispute in the 1800s. The town laid low for the next several years, sending off its sons to fight World War I and then II, and welcoming them back home for better or for worse. But no one in Texarkana was prepared for the national attention that came in the spring of 1946. On February 22nd, 1946, a masked serial killer, dubbed the "Phantom Killer" by the *Texarkana Gazette*'s Calvin Sutton, began terrorizing young couples on the town's secluded country roads.

Today, if you search the Internet for information on Texarkana and its morbid history, you will likely be redirected to pages on *The Town That Dreaded Sundown* and its Arkansan producer, Charles B. Pierce. In 1977, decades after the last murders, this film joined the ranks of *Halloween* and *The Texas Chainsaw Massacre* as one of Hollywood's classic horrors, featuring countless local residents as set extras. While the film's accuracy is something to be questioned, it remains a key piece of the town's identity. Visitors can even catch a screening every Halloween at Spring Lake Park, not far from where one of the infamous murders took place.

Texarkana may have embraced its celebrity status, but eighty years ago the town was paralyzed in fear. Within a single spring, five were dead and three were wounded. All in what had previously been a quiet, friendly community.

A Masked Attacker

Just before midnight, on February 22nd, 1946, Jimmy Hollis and Mary Jeanne Larey were finishing up their date in the backseat of Hollis' father's car. Hollis, 24, and Larey, 19, had been dating for a while, but his parents expected the car (and the lovebirds) home by midnight. Throwing caution to the wind, they parked on a secluded dirt road, known as a lovers' lane, and proceeded to do what young couples will do.

The pair was soon startled by a flashlight, shining through the driver side window and blinding them to whoever stood outside. Hollis quickly composed himself and opened the door, thinking they were being interrupted by an ill-timed police patrol or a prank from some local kids, but they found themselves face-to-face with a masked man holding a gun.

Hollis continued to confront the intruder, telling him, "Fellow, you've got me mixed up with someone else. You got the wrong man." Hollis later said that the masked man muttered something like, "I don't want to kill you, so do what I say." Hollis attempted to calm the assailant, who forced the young man out of the vehicle and demanded Hollis remove his pants, gun pointed squarely at his face. Larey pleaded with Hollis to do as the man said, thinking he would not become violent if they did as he said. Instead the masked man overpowered Hollis, beating him over the head with the revolver. As Hollis lay limp on the cold ground, the attack continued until the sound of Hollis' skull cracking echoed throughout the clearing.

At this point Larey was hysterical with panic, thinking the loud crack of Hollis' broken skull was the sound of him being shot. She told the man they had no money or valuables, attempting to hand the man Hollis' wallet, but he only screamed, "Liar," at her and demanded her purse. Then the masked man told her to run toward the road. Larey ran as fast as she could, but the strange man pursued, continuing to scream, "Liar," at her as she ran.

The assailant eventually outpaced Larey, and forced her to the ground. Larey reported that the man did not rape her, but that assaulted her violent and used his gun to sexually molest her. Larey was afraid for her life, fighting against the weight of her attacker. She eventually managed to escape his grasp, rising up and telling him, "Go ahead and kill me." She then ran to a nearby house at 805 Blanton Street, where she managed to wake up the sleeping woners and pleaded for help. Shortly after, the Bowie County Sheriff, W.H. "Bill" Presley, arrived at what would be the first known Phantom Killer crime scene.

Hollis and Larey were lucky enough to survive this first attack, though they were left with plenty of physical and emotional scars to show for it. Hollis and Larey described their attacker as a tall man wearing a burlap sack with two slits cut for the eyes, though they could not agree on the man's race. Hollis believed the man was white, with tanned skin from working outdoors, while Larey insisted he was a black man because of his mannerisms and "curses." At this point, the attack was treated as a random attempted robbery, it was unknown the chaos that the Phantom Killer would bring in coming months.

The First Kill

In the early hours of March 24th, a truck driver spotted a young man asleep in an Oldsmobile parked on the side of the road. Concerned about the danger of passing traffic, the truck driver ran up to the window, hoping to wake the man and advise him of a better resting area. To the truck driver's horror, the young man was not asleep; he had been shot twice in the back of the head and sat dead in the driver's seat. In the Oldsmobile's backseat was a teenage girl wrapped in a bloody blanket, her body was completely lifeless. These young lovers were not as lucky as the Phantom Killer's first victims.

Richard Griffin, 29, was a retired Navy SeaBee on a double date with his girlfriend of six weeks, Polly Ann Moore, 17, when they pulled over on the highway to have some time alone. They had just finished up dinner with Griffin's sister and her boyfriend at a local café, and

Griffin was in no rush to return his girlfriend to her parents' house. Unfortunately, they would never make it home.

Sometime that previous night, Griffin and Moore had pulled over onto the side of the road. It is believed they were approached similarly to the Phantom Killer's first victims, with a blinding flashlight and pointed gun. There was a heavy rainfall over Texarkana that night, so no one would have been out and about to see the killings take place.

Griffin was likely killed first, with two shots from a .32 Colt revolver to the back of his head. Moore, however, had been dragged from the vehicle and sexually assaulted on the cold, wet ground by their attacker. Blood and marks littered the dirt next to the vehicle. After this horror, Moore was also shot and killed by the Phantom Killer. The assailant pulled a blanket from the car's trunk and wrapped her in it before placing her body in the backseat of the Oldsmobile. Any fingerprints and footprints left behind by the killer that night was washed away by the storm.

Griffin's pockets were found empty and turned inside out, and Moore's purse remained at the scene but was emptied of any cash. With the only apparent motive being robbery, questions still remained as to why the crime was carried out so violently. The *Texarkana Gazette*, at the insistence of the Sheriff Bill Presley, made an announcement on March 27th asking residents to not spread rumors or anything else that they did not see with their own two eyes. Despite offering a cash reward, no solid tips ever made it to the police force.

Murder in the Park

Betty Jo Booker, 15, was a straight-A student who was adored by those around her. She worked with Jerry Atkins playing saxophone for a local band, The Rhythmaires, every Saturday night at the local VFW club. On April 14th, she and Atkins, as well as the rest of their band mates, were playing one of their normal shows. Every other weekend, Atkins gave Booker a ride home alternating with a band mate named Ernie Holcomb. This night was Holcomb's night to drive her home, but Booker told Holcomb not to bother because she had a ride set up with an old classmate who was visiting, Paul Martin. Atkins never knew of this change of plans, and until he received a call the next morning he assumed Booker had left with Holcombe, as usual.

Martin's 1946 Ford Coupe was found at 6:30 the next morning by the Weaver family, who were on their way through Texarkana to Prescott, Arkansas. The keys were found still in the car's ignition. Several miles away, in Spring Lake Park, their bodies would be found. Neither the car nor their bodies were anywhere near their destination that night.

Band and classmates claimed that the two were never close to being a couple, and that Booker felt obligated to go out with Martin because of their connection at school. However, no one knows what they were doing pulled over that night, or why they were in that area of town in the first place. No matter what the true story was that night, Booker and Martin would be the Phantom Killer's third and fourth victims.

Like the previous attack, both victims were shot and killed with a .32 Colt semi-automatic revolver. And like the female targets before her, Booker had been sexually assaulted before her murder. After news of the murder was released, hundreds of Texarkana residents flooded the park, hoping to catch a glimpse of the crime scene or help the investigation.

Martin's body was found almost a mile and a half from the abandoned car. He had been shot four times and the ground surrounding his body was covered in his blood.

Booker's body would not be found until five hours later, over three miles from where the car had been found. Booker was found by the Boyd family and Ted Schoeppey, who had joined the community search party to help find the two teenage victims. Booker had been shot twice, and was found with her hand in her coat pocket.

Both bodies showed signs of a struggle against their attacker, yet their fight was unsuccessful. There was no conclusive evidence as to why their bodies were so far from their car.

Booker's missing saxophone played in the running theory of robbery as a primary motive. The police had alerts al over the area, asking people to keep an eye out for a pawned or for sale saxophone matching the serial number of Booker's, and for several months it was considered one of the best leads the authorities had on finding the killer. Unfortunately for the police, on October 24th, six months after Booker's murder, P. V. Ward and J. F. McNief found the saxophone still in its leather case, just yards from where Booker's body had been found. Ward claimed to know what it was as soon as they stumbled upon it. By the time the case and instrument were turned over to the police, the case had already been labeled closed.

A Red Herring

Public panic over the Phantom Killer was at its all-time high when Virgil and Katie Starks were attacked in their modest farmhouse just ten miles out of town. However, questions would eventually emerge over whether this was truly the work of the Phantom Killer, or if someone else was responsible for the crime.

On the quiet night of May 3rd, Virgil, 36, was reading the Texarkana Gazette when two gunshots burst through the front window of their ranch-style home. These bullets hit Virgil in the head, killing him instantly. Katie was lying in bed, already dressed in her nightgown, when she heard the sound of breaking glass. She headed for the living room, where her husband had been seated, only to find him slumped in his armchair, dead. She cried in fear as she reached for the phone, but the attacker shot through her lower jaw, spraying teeth fragments across the Starks kitchen.

In a state of panic and extreme pain, Katie managed to get back up to her feet. She attempted to grab her husband's gun, but was disoriented from being shot. Despite her injuries, she escaped from the house and ran for her sister's down the street. Finding the house empty, she continued to her neighbors' until she found refuge in the Prater house, where the police were finally called. When A. V. Prater answered the door, Katie simply said, "Virgil's dead," before collapsing on the ground. In the time it took for the police to arrive the killer had fled, taking no valuables or anything else of note with him.

Initially, this attack was labeled as another of the Phantom Killer's. It followed the same time pattern as his previous attacks, used a gun as the primary weapon, and targeted a couple. One of the biggest pieces of evidence connecting this attack to the Phantom Killer was a set of unfamiliar tire tracks that matched those found at the other crime scenes. Because of these similarities, many citizens of Texarkana insist that this murder and attempted assault was the Phantom Killer's final blow to the small town's community.

In November 1948, the local authorities made a different conclusion. Another man was arrested and charged with the home invasion and attack on Virgil and Katie Starks. Law enforcement referenced several reasons as to this not being the work of the Phantom Killer, including the fact that the weapon used was a .22 rifle. This change in weapon, as well as the fact this was a home invasion earlier in the evening, pointed police to consider a different suspect entirely.

The town is still home to many skeptics who believe this attack was the Phantom Killer's doing. The crime scene at the Starks home was filled with physical DNA evidence, but at the time DNA testing was only beginning to emerge in the most developed areas of the nation. A little town like Texarkana was nowhere near equipped to handle a case like this, and the DNA evidence was discarded or improperly stored for later testing. While the official stance is that the Phantom Killer was not involved in this attack, the question still haunts many in the area.

A Town In Panic

As the attacks added up, tension in the town of Texarkana grew. After the first and second attack, police forces from both states increased patrols on the town's secluded back roads. A community that had once been friendly, where front doors were never locked and neighbors were always welcome, now grew eerily quiet after sundown.

Businesses saw a decline in customers, especially those catering to the night crowd. Residents were afraid to leave home, even during the daylight, for fear they may become the next target of the Phantom Killer. However, one industry in town became a hotspot for concerned citizens – the local hardware and ammo shops.

Residents bought up guns and ammo like crazy, hoping to be able to defend themselves from the attacks. Deadbolts and other home security devices became commonplace in all the towns households, and some homeowners were even seen setting up booby traps and other contraptions to catch the killer in his tracks.

Many of the town's local high school and college boys rounded up patrol groups. These men would go out at night with baseball bats and other makeshift weapons, hoping to catch the Phantom Killer on the prowl. None of them were ever successful.

Rumors continued to spread and impair the investigations. There was constant news about someone's son being arrested for the murders, or a suspect being charged, but these rumors rarely ever revealed themselves to be true. Police were forced to perform damage control on the stories spreading around town while also conducting their own investigation into the attacks.

Under the Spotlight

After the final attack, at the Starks farmhouse, authorities and media swarmed into Texarkana like never before. The quiet town was buzzing with news reporters from all across the nation, and reports of the murders were spreading to all areas of the country. Texarkana had never experienced the media's curious eye before.

The famous Texas Rangers stepped into the investigation, headed by the well-known Manuel "Lone Wolf" Gonzaullas. Gonzaullas was the first Ranger captain from Spanish descent, and was known for being a ruthless charmer in his day. He spent a great of his time providing interviews for national newspapers and radio broadcasts about the state of the investigation. He was even found one day taking pictures of the Starks crime scene with a young *Life* magazine reporter; neighbors had reported suspicious lights and sounds from the house when Gonzaullas and the woman were found.

While the local press, headed by the Texarkana Gazette, dubbed the suspected serial killer the "Phantom Killer" or "Phantom Slayer," national media clung to a different name: "The Moonlight Murderer." Because of this title, many believe that the murders were all committed under the full moon, when the nights were in fact at their darkest during the time of the crimes.

A Fruitless Investigation

The entire nation was on the lookout for a masked killer terrorizing young couples, with leads coming in from all areas of the South. In all, the authorities considered over four hundred separate suspects, but no one was ever charged with the attacks of that spring. While most of these suspects never received any public attention, the media caught wind of some of the more notable ones.

A middle-aged man from College Station, a Texas town several miles west of Texarkana, was at one point considered a prime suspect. He had previously been caught sneaking up on parked cars, typically with young couples inside, and brandishing a .22 rifle in order to threaten and rob them. While this man was never convicted of murder, many believed him to be the Phantom Killer based on the similar crime and weapon.

In Fayetteville, a young male graduate student of the University of Arkansas committed suicide. In the wake of his untimely death, a note was found containing a handwritten poem and confession to the murders in Texarkana. His military records showed he had showed "homosexual tendencies" during his time with the U.S. Navy, and at the time these tendencies were believed to be a mental disorder related to sexual crimes like rape or assault. Nothing of value ever came from this lead.

Several local residents accused an IRS agent of the crimes, seemingly because of his antisocial demeanor or because he had gotten on the town's bad side. Another man claimed to have committed the crimes during fits of amnesia. Neither of these claims resulted in an arrest.

In 1999 and 2000, several years after the last murder, an anonymous woman called surviving family members of the Phantom Killer's victims, claiming to be his daughter. She apologized for the actions of his crimes and begged for forgiveness from the families. There is speculation over whether these claims are valid, but many believe them to simply be a cry for attention. After all, the primary suspect of the Phantom Killer murders, Youell Swinney, never had a daughter.

Chasing a Criminal

During his time investigating the Moonlight Murders, Max Tackett, an Arkansas law officer, made a puzzling connection. Before each murder a car had been reported stolen and subsequently abandoned on the side of the rode. This information led police to believe that the Phantom Killer was using stolen vehicles to flee the crime scenes, and then dumping them before disappearing into the night.

The next car reported stolen triggered a police stakeout, with law enforcement hoping to find the killer connected to the vehicle. As police closed in on the stolen vehicle, Peggy Swinney was found to be driving. Police seized the car and took Peggy into custody, where she was questioned on how she came to possess the stolen vehicle.

Peggy revealed that Youell Swinney, a known car thief in Texarkana, had given the car to her, but that wasn't all she had to say. Peggy began telling police how Youell was the Phantom Killer, how he had assaulted and murdered all those couples, and how he had made her promise not to tell anyone. She included details of the crimes that had not been given to the public, information only known by police and the killer himself.

Before the police could move in on Youell Swinney, Peggy's story changed. She claimed that her previous confession was a lie, and that Youell was not the Phantom Killer after all. Eventually law enforcement discovered that Peggy and Youell had recently been married, making her unable to testify against her husband at all. While Youell remained an unofficial suspect, it seemed that the police were unable to touch him. But that changed in 1947, when Youell was arrested for auto theft.

At that time, Youell Swinney already had a long criminal record. He had been previously charged with counterfeiting, burglary, and assault, landing him in the Texas State Penitentiary for many years. After his release, he continued his work as a career criminal, but avoided capture for the time being.

During the investigation, police found evidence that Youell had owned a .32 Colt revolver, the murder weapon used to kill the second and third sets of victims, but that he had recently lost the gun in a failed card game. In hi home was also a shirt with the name "Stark" embroidered on the pocket, but it is unknown whether this shirt was actually connected to the Starks murder in the previous year.

With Youell in custody for auto theft, the police attempted to pin him as Texarkana's Phantom Killer. The man had a history of violence and sexual assault, and the record of stolen cars pointed toward his involvement in the murders. Youell never denied his innocence; he simply stayed quiet and refused to work with the police when questioned. A botched injection of "truth serum" during an interview in Little Rock, Arkansas, would eventually end the authorities' questioning of Youell regarding the Moonlight Murders. He was placed in prison for auto theft.

Youell remained in prison until 1973. Many of his cellmates recounted stories that Youell had told them, ones that included intimate details of the Phantom Killer's murder scenes and heavily suggested that Youell knew more than he let on. In 1994, Youell died a free man, never admitting to the Texarkana murders. To this day, most consider Swinney to be the Phantom Killer, even if he never served time for these crimes.

The Missing Woman

On June 1st, 1948, 21-year-old Virginia Carpenter departed Texarkana by train, on her way to her first semester of studying at the Texas State College for Women. She left Union Station at about 3PM, and headed for Denton, Texas and her new life as an educated woman. On the train ride, she met another student by the name of Marjorie Webster, who she shared a taxi with on the way to their dormitories.

Their taxi driver, Edgar Ray "Jack" Zachary, first dropped off Webster at the Fitzgerald dormitories, and then continued on to Brackenridge Hall, where Carpenter would be staying for the term. Zachary reported seeing Carpenter approach two young men in a yellow convertible outside the dorm, saying that she seemed to recognize them and was excited to see them. The next day, Zachary returned to the dorms to deliver some of Carpenter's luggage that she had forgotten at the station. He placed the trunk at the hall's front entrance and left, but no one ever claimed the luggage. That previous night would be the last time Virginia Carpenter was seen.

On June 4th, Carpenter's boyfriend, Kenny Branham, and her mother reported Virginia missing. After being brushed off by authorities, Mrs. Carpenter and other family members left for Denton late in the evening, hoping to help the police find Virginia.

Within several days, there were airplanes, motorboats, and on-foot search parties scanning the surrounding area for any sign of Virginia. Drivers of yellow convertibles were stopped and questioned, and Zachary was questioned by police and subjected to a polygraph test. Carpenter quickly became one of the most famous missing person cases in Texas, with her picture circulating across the country.

Before long, rumors started spreading back in Texarkana. Virginia Carpenter had personally known three of the Phantom Killer's victims, and some started to believe that she had a target on her back. Perhaps the killer had followed her from Texarkana to Denton, just another passenger on the crowded train. Or perhaps the killer was someone that Carpenter knew, like one of the men seen in the yellow convertible to night she went missing. Either way, many believe that this disappearance was connected to the attacks in 1946.

Countless sightings of Carpenter across Texas - riding in a car, buying groceries, or hitchhiking - continued to flow in, but no solid leads were ever discovered. By 1955, Carpenter was considered dead. She had been missing for seven years, and little hope remained of finding her. Despite this, tips continued to emerge on Carpenter's possible whereabouts.

In 1959, a wooden box was found buried with female remains inside that matched Carpenter's physical description. They were sent to Austin for examination, but the landowners soon confessed to digging them up from an old cemetery.

In 1998, a man called the police claiming to know where Carpenter's body was buried. He led police to the grounds of the Texas State College for Women, the school she was meant to attend, but the search came up empty.

Carpenter's disappearance causes some to doubt Youell Swinney's guilt. If her disappearance was a result of the Phantom Killer, the same man who brutally attacked at least three different couples, then this man could not be Swinney. At the time Carpenter went missing, Swinney was being held in prison for auto theft. Maybe Peggy Swinney had a hand in the disappearance of Carpenter, or her abduction was committed by someone other than the Phantom Killer, but it could not have been Swinney.

Phantoms Around the World

Some believe that the Phantom Killer simply moved his crimes to a new location, but it is likely he just inspired other killers to follow his pattern of attack. As the United States reached the height of violent crime and serial killers, attacks cropped up across the country and even abroad. The Phantom Kiiler's *modus operandi* (or M.O.) would become commonplace among serial killers in the coming decades, including the Zodiac Killer, Il Mostro, and the Son of Sam.

In 1946, a young couple was shot in Fort Lauderdale, Florida. Elaine Eldridge and Lawrence Hogan were parked outside Dania Beach when someone approached the vehicle and shot both victims with a .32 semi-automatic handgun. While the weapon used was not a Colt, it remained very similar to the one used in Texarkana. No fingerprints or footprints were found at the scene. With several similarities to the Texarkana attacks, many believed that the killer had relocated across the country. Texas, Arkansas, and Florida police worked together on the investigation, but no major connections were ever revealed to the public.

Located in San Francisco, the Zodiac Killer operated very similarly to the Phantom Killer during the late 1960s. He stalked young people in their vehicles and shot them with a revolver, and his identity remains unknown. However, unlike the Phantom Killer who personally avoided the media's attention, the Zodiac Killer was hungry for exposure. His main source of fame comes from sending cryptic notes to the Bay Area press, including four ciphers. Only one of these ciphers was ever solved, but it led the police no closer to identifying a suspect. These notes were examined top to bottom, in hopes of finding the true identity of the Zodiac Killer, but no leads were ever found.

Across the Atlantic Ocean, from 1968 to 1985, Florence, Italy was shook by sixteen murders. Dubbed Il Mostro or The Monster of Florence, the killer shot young couples parked alone in their cars with a .22 rifle. While four different suspects were arrested and charged with these murders throughout the years, the investigation has attracted scrutiny and many believe these men were actually innocent.

While the Son of Sam's identity is known today, his killings reflected those of the Phantom Killer and others. Operating in New York City in the mid 1970s, David Berkowitz killed six victims with a .44 Bulldog revolver. His attacks triggered the biggest manhunt in New York City, and for years women kept their hair short and avoided disco clubs for fear of being Berkowitz's next target. Like the Zodiac Killer, Berkowitz loved taunting the police and media with cryptic letters, where he promised to continue killing until he was caught. After his capture in 1977, Berkowitz enjoyed a bit of morbid celebrity for his crimes, which many reported he seemed to enjoy greatly. He remains in prison today, serving six life sentences.

While it is unlikely that the Phantom Killer actually relocated to be the Zodiac Killer or Il Mostro, some true crime experts believe it is possible. While the Phantom Killer was one of the first of his kind, looking back his killings were not exceptionally unique by today's standards.

It is easy to see how the Phantom Killer and his Moonlight Murders have shaped our ideas of killers today. Urban legends of a mad man stalking young couples in love, scratching on car doors and leaving bloody hooks behind, persist around campfires and in dark corners of the Internet. *The Town That Dreaded Sundown* might live among the likes of Freddy Krueger and Michael Myers, but it is a fictionalized retelling of the very real horrors that haunted Texarkana that year.

THE MURDER OF AMY ALLWINE

JESSI DIXON

In May 2016, a team of hackers cracked into a site on the dark web – and unknowingly uncovered evidence that would eventually help investigators with the FBI solve the murder of a woman named Amy Allwine.

"If you want to kill someone, or to beat the shit out of him, we are the right guys," read the homepage of Besa Mafia, a website that was supposedly affiliated with an Albanian organized crime ring. In exchange for bitcoin, they claimed they would arrange beatings and even assassinations. The site had appealed to many potential clients, including a user named "dogdaygod."

The FBI determined that "dogdaygod" was responsible for arranging the murder of Amy Allwine, a church-going Midwestern woman. "Dogdaygod" wanted the slaying to "look like an accident," according to the emails sent to Besa Mafia. The user claimed Amy Allwine "tore my family apart by sleeping with my husband, and is stealing clients from my business."

However, this portrayal of Amy Allwine didn't fit with the victim's life. The 43 year old dog trainer ran her own business in a suburb outside of St. Paul, Minnesota. She'd met her husband, Stephen, at a Christian college, and the couple had continued to pursue their dedication to their faith as active members of a local congregation of the United Church of God. Stephen even served as church elder, providing marriage counselling services to couples who were struggling to stay together. The couple even raised an adopted son.

"Amy was the most motivating person, she was the most positive person," said Jennifer Waters, one of Amy's dog training students. "She had nothing but good things to say about anybody."

Friends and family described Amy as a loving, devoted mother and a compassionate, dedicated friend. She seemed hardly to be the kind of woman "dogdaygod" insisted that she was, but it looked like someone was trying to have her killed.

In July 2016, a woman who called herself Jane sent Amy Allwine the first of two untraceable emails containing threats and insults. Jane said Amy was a "fat bitch" who had destroyed the woman's marriage, and more disturbingly, threatened Amy's family and her son – using details that clearly gave the impression that Jane had the Allwines under surveillance.

"Here is how you can save your family," read Jane's initial email. "Commit suicide."

The email went on to assure Amy that if she did not comply with the sender's instructions to kill herself, she would "slowly see things taken away from you, and each time you will know that you could have stopped it." It also included a list of suggested methods Amy could employ to carry out the grisly deed.

Around the same time, the FBI reached out to the Cottage Grove police department, advising them of the murder-for-hire plot where some unknown user was planning to pay virtual currency to have Amy killed. The police met with the Allwines and recommended they step up their home security. And they did – Stephen even received a permit to carry a handgun on August 10, and purchased a 9mm Springfield XDS to protect his wife.

But just months later, that same gun would be used to kill her.

Murder for hire

The plot to kill Amy appears to have originated on Valentine's Day, according to a timeline later pieced together by investigators from the FBI, Cottage Grove police, and the Minnesota Bureau of Criminal Apprehension. On February 14, 2016, "dogdaygod" attempted to pay $5,000 to have Amy Allwine killed in a car crash.

The user provided Besa Mafia with plenty of information to help them make the murder look like an accident – details of her travel schedule and constant whereabouts. Meanwhile, "dogdaygod" was also searching the dark web for different ways to launder virtual currency like bitcoin to pay for the assassination.

It was the 35-character bitcoin address that police would eventually find on the smartphone of Stephen Allwine – linking Amy's devoted Christian husband to the assassination plot. But the hit man had been unable to follow through with the kill, and police had discovered something else on Stephen's smartphone.

Apparently, the church elder had some dark secrets. Stephen had spent a few months involved in a relationship with a woman he'd met on Ashley Madison – a website specifically for people looking for extramarital affairs. Michelle, Stephen told police, was from the "western metro Twin Cities" area, and investigators were able to locate her.

"She stated that the two had an intimate relationship for several months during which time they took out-of-town trips together, as well as spent time together locally," the police report read. "She admitted their affair was sexual in nature and provided photographs of the two of them together in which they are hugging and kissing."

This wasn't the first woman Stephen Allwine met on Ashley Madison, however. Police also learned that he had gone on a date with another woman in October 2015, whom he met for dinner at a nearby golf course. The evening ended with a kiss, but they never saw each other again.

Michelle, though, maintained an ongoing relationship with Stephen. She recalled instances when Amy was out of town that Stephen had asked her to come to his home, but that she needed to sneak in the back way to avoid being detected by the home security system. The photographs Michelle shared with authorities were from December 2015, and she said the romance "fizzled" by February – around the same time as "dogdaygod" started investigating the possibility of having Amy Allwine killed by an anonymous hit man from Besa Mafia.

Michelle also told police that if the murder-for-hire plot was true, Stephen Allwine was certainly intelligent enough to pull it off.

According to authorities, the murder scene had been staged to look like a suicide – perhaps an attempt to make it look like Amy had given in to the threats that had been emailed to her from the purported woman named Jane. However, investigators determined that Amy Allwine's death was "inconsistent" with suicide, and charged her husband Stephen with the premeditated murder.

"She's probably dead."

It was Stephen who placed the 911 call on November 13, 2016 – informing the dispatcher that he had arrived home with their nine year old son to find his wife dead in their home. Their son had spotted the body first and brought it to Stephen's attention, which is when he called 911.

When police arrived at approximately 7 p.m., pumpkins were roasting in the kitchen – but Stephen and his son were waiting for police in the open garage. He directed officers to the location of his wife's body, in the bedroom. According to the charging document, Amy was lying on the floor with a pool of blood under her head. Although her body was still warm to the touch, the responding officers were unable to detect a pulse. Later, they would state that Amy was "obviously dead."

Lying near Amy's left forearm and elbow was a gun – a 9mm Springfield XDS. According to Amy's parents, she was right handed.

Additionally, police couldn't find any stippling, or powder burns, on her head, indicating that the gun hadn't been against her head when it went off. There was also no gunpowder, soot, or even blood spatter on Amy's hands.

Investigators discovered traces of Amy's blood elsewhere in the house, though, despite evidence that parts of the home had been cleaned recently. Remnants of bloody footprints were uncovered leading back and forth between the kitchen and the bedroom, and detectives determined that it appeared to be evidence of an "attempted cleanup."

"Agents also found nine separate areas of visible transfer stains and bloodlike substance present on the floor between the master bedroom and laundry room, darkest near the bedroom and progressively lighter near the laundry room," the police document read. "These appeared to be bloody footprints, and were only visible when the crime scene team used luminol and not to the naked eye."

Additional footprints were traced throughout the residence – outside the master bedroom, between the couch and kitchen island, between the dining room table and basement door, in the hallway, in the main floor bathroom, and in the child's bedroom. However, the team noted that "the bloody footprints were not found near any access point to the residence except the garage access door."

Despite the numerous security features that had been added to the house since Cottage Grove police had told the Allwines about the virtual threat on Amy's life, there was no evidence that an outside attacker had killed Stephen's wife. He was the only person coming and going from the property, according to footage captured by the security cameras, and authorities found no signs of forced entry.

Just days after the murder, Stephen Allwine was asked specifically about the blood that appeared to have been cleaned up prior to the arrival of the initial responders. He told detectives that he "had no information about this," adding that no one had been previously injured in the home.

According to Stephen, Amy hadn't been feeling well on the day of her death. She'd mentioned being light-headed, but hadn't wanted to see the doctor about it. According to the Allwines' son, who had been at his grandparents' house when Amy was killed, she was feeling dizzy and his father was going to take her to a clinic.

The last time Stephen saw Amy, he told police, was at around 5:30 p.m., when he left to pick up their son to take him to a gym class. Stephen worked in information technology and had two employers, but worked out of a home office in the basement of the family's home

– a regular shift from 6 a.m. until 5 p.m. from Sunday through Wednesday.

On November 13, detectives learned that Stephen had logged in for work at 6:24 a.m., and remained active until 12:13. He took a lunch break of just more than 41 minutes, and at around 2 p.m., called his in-laws to see if they could pick up their son so that he could get more work done. He said he checked on Amy a couple of times throughout the day, and at around 5 p.m., she said she was fine.

At around 5:30, Stephen left the house to pick up the couple's son from Amy's parents' home. He said he intended to bring the child to a gym class that evening, but while filling his vehicle up with gas, he realized he had forgotten his son's gym shorts at home. Instead of going to the gym, he took his son for dinner at Culver's.

Once they arrived back at the house, the child saw his mother's body in the bedroom and asked Stephen why she was sleeping on the floor. Then, he told police, Stephen replied, "she's probably dead," and called 911.

The home security system that the Allwines had installed in the home was set to record the dates and times that the front and garage doors are opened. On November 13, police learned that after Stephen said he left to pick up his son, no one entered or exited the home until Stephen and the child returned.

"Most notably," the police document stated, "the search warrant return also revealed that after (Amy)'s father left the residence at 2:02 p.m., the service door was opened at 2:40 p.m., 2:42 p.m., and 4:40 p.m."

In the statement he made to police, Stephen claimed that once his son had been picked up by his grandfather, he had been working in the basement until he left at 5:26 p.m. But Stephen's employer reported that after his lunch break on November 13, he did not re-enter the phone queue to finish his shift, and didn't enter any case updates that day – "despite the fact that (Stephen) works on customer issues and is supposed to log all of his activity in his case notes."

Stephen's other employer verified that he didn't log in at all on November 13.

Police noted that Stephen's home office contained "a large amount of computer equipment, which appeared to be very sophisticated and technologically advanced" – however, Stephen had denied having any knowledge about hacking or the dark web in his statement. Instead, he said he knows "how things are supposed to work in the legitimate world."

Investigators quickly learned that Stephen had not been truthful with law enforcement regarding his activity on the internet – information gleaned from examining Stephen's computer revealed that he'd been accessing the dark web since as early as 2014.

Absolute determination

After initially reaching out to Besa Mafia on February 15, the user named "dogdaygod" posted on March 6 that "she" needs "this bitch dead." Amy would be traveling to Moline, Illinois, with a companion, on March 19 and 20 – and according to the post "dogdaygod" made on the website, they didn't care if the companion was killed in the hit, as well. Investigators learned that Amy Allwine had indeed traveled to Moline during that time, when she attended a dog training competition.

However, "dogdaygod" was informed on March 20 that the Besa Mafia hitman had not had the opportunity to kill Amy in Moline – leading the user to suggest that Besa Mafia send someone to complete the hit a few weeks later, when Amy would be in Atlanta. Besa Mafia recommended the use of a sniper for an additional ten bitcoin, or approximately $12,000.

"It was ultimately decided between 'dogdaygod' and Besa Mafia that (Amy) would be killed at her home and the house would be burned afterward," stated police documents. "Besa Mafia stated that with the additional ten bitcoin cost, the plan had a 100 per cent success rate. 'Dogdaygod' agreed to provide the money by the next day."

On March 22, "Dogdaygod" attempted to transfer the bitcoin, and provided Besa Mafia with a specific 34-digit alphanumeric address to be matched with the transfer. According to investigators, these bitcoin addresses are considered unique to each transaction – and during a computer forensics search of Stephen's computer, the specific bitcoin address "dogdaygod" had posted was located on a backed up deleted file – "linking (Stephen) directly to 'dogdaygod.'"

Still, though, Besa Mafia's hitman hadn't completed the job. "Dogdaygod" was informed that their hitman had been caught driving a stolen vehicle and had been taken to jail, but according to local police, "no one was apprehended in Minnesota and western Wisconsin and was arrested in a stolen vehicle and in possession of a gun" during this time. But Besa Mafia didn't stop soliciting money from the user, putting off the hit again and again.

"We have zero information at this point that any of the hits that were ordered on that website were actually carried out," a Minnesota detective told Fox 9 news. "In fact, there is pretty good evidence, I think, that it was just a scam."

In May, Besa Mafia was targeted by an ethical hacker, who published the site's customer list and revealed that the entire operation was a scam. The FBI payed close attention and began investigating the site – while "dogdaygod" had to seek out an alternative solution.

The user popped up on another dark web site looking for a drug dealer in the Minneapolis area – and a forensic search of Stephen Allwine's phone revealed cookies from search engines used to search the dark web were installed on his phone at the same time.

The FBI discovered that "dogdaygod" had been trying to access a drug called scopolamine, or "devil's breath." A derivative of nightshade that can be administered as a powder with no discernable flavour or odor, scopolamine is primarily used to treat nausea. However, the drug is also known to erase a person's memory, according to police documents, and "rendering them incapable of exercising their free will."

While investigating the murder of Amy Allwine, police asked the Ramsey County medical examiner's office to test for the presence of scopolamine – and found that the drug was present in her system, at more than 45 times the concentration of a prescription. Amy had never been prescribed the drug.

"It should be noted that a search of (Amy)'s iPhone 6 revealed that on November 13, 2016, it was last used to search 'Vertigo-Wikipedia' at approximately 2:01 p.m.," police documents stated.

Her time of death was estimated by the medical examiner to have been around 3 p.m. – approximately four hours before police were called. Stephen claimed he'd last seen her and spoken to her more than two hours after the estimated time of death, at around 5:30 p.m. He'd gone into the room to tell Amy that he was leaving to pick up their son, and had found her kneeling by the bed.

"(Stephen) stated that he assumed she was praying, which was not unusual," the police report read. "(Stephen) stated before he left, he asked (Amy) how she was feeling, and she stated she was feeling okay."

"A cold and calculating killer."

Within months, police had gathered enough evidence to link Stephen Allwine to the "dogdaygod" account – and alleged that he had killed his wife after Besa Mafia had failed to complete the ordered hit. Prosecutors claimed he'd been motivated by a mix of religious guilt and piety, as divorce was simply not an option for a church elder who regularly provided marriage counselling.

"He was seeing other women, but he didn't want to divorce (Amy) because of his position in the church," the jury was told by Washington County assistant attorney Jamie Lynn Kreuser.

As members of the United Church of God, the Allwines took a conservative stance on marriage and divorce. According to the church's website, marriage is a "commitment for life" where no "recognized troubles" can justify divorcing a mate "with the freedom to remarry."

"Who would want to do this?" asked Kreuser, noting that as a caring mother, dog owner, and woman of faith, Amy Allwine was not the sort of person who would choose to die by suicide. "Someone who didn't want to be married to her anymore."

The incredible lengths Stephen allegedly went to in order to ensure his wife's death also demonstrated a significant level of sophistication, which was noted by Washington County prosecutor Fred A. Fink Jr. He said Stephen's action "appears to be an absolute determination to kill this woman."

Stephen was also the sole benefactor of his wife's $700,000 life insurance policy, prosecutors said.

But the defense argued that there was insufficient physical evidence connecting Stephen with the crime – all forensics had been able to find was a "particle characteristic of gunshot residue" on Stephen's right hand from the sample he'd given to police after Amy's death.

According to Stephen's attorney, Kevin DeVore, prosecutors had built a case on "theories with gaps," and incorporated plenty of speculation to "bridge those gaps."

"It sounds like an amazing story – but it's not a TV show or a movie, but real life," he said. "Just because he had an affair doesn't mean he killed his wife or even didn't love his wife."

The jury disagreed with the defense's argument, despite Fink's own admission that the case was "entirely circumstantial." On January 31, 2018, after just eight hours of deliberation, they found Stephen Allwine guilty of first-degree murder for the premeditated attack on his wife.

Addressing the courtroom at his sentencing just days later, Stephen stated that he had always loved his wife and did not kill her – adding, "I've never asked for anything except to work for God."

"I never went to sleep, and I never woke up without kissing her," he said. "The grief of losing her is tremendous."

He also claimed that the couple had never even argued, noting that "no one ever talked bad about our relationship." During his statement, he insinuated that an unknown assailant had entered the house through a patio door which had been left unlocked.

"Even though she's gone, she's gone knowing I loved her," Stephen said. "The only image I have in my mind is one of my smiling, beautiful wife."

Judge B. William Ekstrum was unable to conceal his irritation, and told Stephen, "you are an incredible actor, a hypocrite, and a cold and calculating killer."

"We're looking at a complete narcissist," Fink added after the sentencing. "His elocution was all about him – not Amy or her death."

"The most complex case."

Ekstrum sentenced Stephen to life in prison with no possibility of parole – the mandatory sentence for a conviction of first degree murder. His term is to be served at St. Cloud Prison. Stephen said that during his time at the Washington County Jail, he's met drug addicts, child molesters, and kidnappers – and had been conducting regular bible study sessions.

"I'm going to take my bible to St. Cloud (Prison)," Stephen said, "and see what happens."

He no longer serves as a church elder, however, as the Council of Elders at the United Church of God removed Stephen from ministry after he was initially charged with Amy's murder in 2017. While the church did release a brief statement following the sentencing, it offered no "speculative comments" regarding the verdict.

"It is our fervent hope that all will continue praying to our merciful Father about the entire situation and be compassionate about what the extended families are going through," the statement read. "We can have confidence that our all-knowing God is aware of all aspects regarding this tragic situation."

Prosecutors were pleased with the result, although Fink noted making the conviction required the jury to almost piece together a "jigsaw puzzle" of evidence.

"We believe the jury did the right thing," he said after the sentence was handed down. "They had a lot of pieces of evidence to go through ... I've been doing this 43 years and it's probably the most complex case I've ever tried. It's fair that this defendant spends the rest of his life in prison."

It was also one of the more complex investigations ever undertaken by Cottage Grove police, according to detective Sgt. Randy McAlister. As many as five detectives worked the case over two months – with the first month requiring them to set aside much of the rest of their workload to focus on the investigation full-time.

"I think the big difference between this and a more common murder the dark web, the internet connection – that's what's really been taking a lot of time," he said. "This is the first case involving death threats on a purported dark web website that we've ever dealt with. This is definitely the most in-depth."

Kreuser said that throughout the sensationalized trial, prosecutors stayed focused on the victim and her loved ones – despite significant media attention.

"At the end of the day, justice was served," she said, "and I'm glad for Amy and her family."

Many of Amy's family and friends provided victim impact statements during the six day trial – though few of these accounts were critical of Stephen. The courtroom was filled with people who knew the couple, either through Amy's business or the family's dedication to the church.

"It was very supportive for the entire thing," said DeVore. "It goes beyond the love one might expect."

Still, Amy's parents were stung by Stephen's betrayal, and called him a "selfish person." They added they'd been "astonished" to hear how Stephen had spent months plotting their daughter's murder – at Amy's wedding twenty years earlier, her father remembered how he "put her hand into Steve's and asked him to take good care of my little girl."

Amy's sister, Julie Brown, told the court about how Amy had "lived in fear every waking moment of the last months of her life," thanks to the anonymous death threats she'd received, and the murder-for-hire plot the FBI had warned her about. Even simple tasks like going grocery shopping "spurred intense anxiety" for Amy.

"We've lost so much," Brown said, "but with God's grace, all is not lost."

After the verdict, Amy's parents and siblings released another statement.

"We can summon no words to describe life without Amy," it read. "We loved her and miss her tremendously. We now turn to the path ahead of privately healing and grieving."

THE VALENTINES DAY MURDER
ANA BENSON

Richard and Stacy Schoeck had a perfect marriage, or at least it looked ideal for their friends and family. Even though they have been together for a long time, they seemed to have eyes only for each other. Richard was Stacy's fifth husband and everyone was certain that he was indeed the love of her life. The couple still went on dates and celebrated their love in every way possible. So when Valentine's Day in 2010 came around, the Schoecks were setting up a romantic little getaway and a card exchange in a picturesque Belton Bridge Park which is located in Lula, Georgia.

Lula is a quiet little tourist town so when their Police Department received a frantic phone call with Stacy on the other end of the line, they knew something serious had happened. The town was shocked to discover that a murder occurred right there in their calm little oasis. But soon enough, the sinister plot started to unravel and the law enforcement realized that things were not as they seemed.

So what made Stacy Schoeck turn on her loving husband and who helped her with the murderous plan?

Early life

Stacy Morgan was born in 1971 in Florida. Her childhood wasn't perfect at all and her father died when she was really young. This left a permanent mark on Stacy even though her mother remarried soon and she did have a father figure in her life. She was also molested during this time frame by an individual who remained anonymous to everyone around her. Stacy grew up to be a lovely teenage girl who would fall in love easily. She met her first husband while she was still in high school and the couple got married shortly after. Unfortunately, he wasn't what Stacy was looking for and it took her two years to come to this conclusion. She filed for a divorce and the two separated.

When Stacy was twenty years old, she met her second husband. Soon after the wedding, Stacy found out that she was pregnant with her first child. The marriage lasted a little more than a year and she once again filed for a divorce when her son was just a toddler. Instead of being beaten down by two failed marriages, Stacy remained strong and made a decision to improve herself. After all, she was only twenty-two years old. She applied for college and got accepted. Stacy moved on to raise her son on her own and earn a degree in psychology and nursing at the same time.

She managed to find the employment as soon as she got out of college. Stacy was still very optimistic about her love life and wanted to find someone to spend the rest of her life with. She met her third husband in 1997 but unfortunately, the marriage was short-lived once again. It lasted for only six weeks. Stacy decided to date casually in the future and gave birth to her second son in 1998. She was still a single mother but this didn't seem to bother her at all.

Stacy did need to improve her financial status and she found a better job opportunity at a clinic which was located in Atlanta. The family moved over there and she was ready to start over. She got an excellent position at the hospital's administration with the possibility of even better promotion. She would assist the doctors on a daily basis with various tasks. Stacy was a successful and independent woman who was capable of taking care of her two small boys on her own.

But something was still missing and Stacy was longing for a partner who would be there for her. She was tired of casual encounters and needed some stability. So in 2001 she married for the fourth time and moved out to a small town near Atlanta. She got pregnant once again and gave birth to her third son. She lived in a large house with her fourth husband and it seemed that her life was absolutely perfect. Her boys were happy and they loved the suburban lifestyle. On the other hand, Stacy was still unhappy. Soon after the separation from her fourth husband in 2005, Stacy met Richard Schoeck, a graphic designer who was slightly older than her. He was a patient at the hospital where Stacy worked at the time. The two hit it off immediately.

Richard Schoeck was an adventurer who lived his life to the maximum. Stacy was immediately attracted to his positive attitude and passionate outlook. Richard accepted Stacy's sons like they were his own and would often organize family outings that included the entire family. She loved how different Richard was from all of her previous husbands and thought that she had finally found the one.

Unconcerned about Stacy's previous failed marriages, Richard still wanted to make their relationship permanent. The couple did get married in 2007 but the ceremony wasn't standard at all. Stacy and Richard eloped and told everyone about the wedding once they came back home. It was in Richard's nature to do something so spontaneous and Stacy adored him for that.

Richard became a stay at home dad after the wedding and he would form a close bond with Stacy's boys. He was very involved with their school and hobbies so he ended up adopting the youngest two. He really did accept this small family as his own and wanted the best for the boys. Everyone approved of Richard and Stacy's family hoped that she finally found the man of her life. Unfortunately, this marriage would end up tragically in just a couple of years.

The murder of Richard Schoeck

Prior to Valentine's Day in February of 2010, Stacy invited Richard on a small romantic getaway to the town of Lulu, Georgia. They were supposed to meet in Belton Bridge Park which is a secluded area near the town itself and exchange gifts there. This wasn't unusual for the Schoecks because they would often go on different adventures that were supposed to spice up their love life. The Police dispatchers received a frantic phone call sometime after the nightfall. Stacy was screaming that her husband was shot and robbed. He wasn't showing any signs of life.

The police arrived at the scene of the crime and sure enough, Richard's body was lying next to his pickup truck. The blood was both inside and outside of the vehicle which meant that several shots were fired. At least one bullet hit him while he was still in the driver's seat or getting out of the car. He crawled out, perhaps to run away or defend himself. The shooter continued firing the gun until they were certain that Richard was dead.

The investigators immediately closed off the area and examined the tire tracks which were visible in the surrounding mud. They noticed that the third vehicle was definitely there and that it left the scene of the crime prior to the arrival of Stacy. The law enforcement marked them as the evidence. However, there were some red flags that indicated that this wasn't a standard robbery. For instance, Richard's valet was still in the car and his jewelry was on him. Nothing was taken from the scene.

Stacy wasn't a suspect at the time but the police escorted her to the station in order to interview her and get as many details as possible. Lulu is a quiet town where crime rarely happens so the law enforcement couldn't zero in on any possible reason why Richard was shot. One theory suggested that he might have interrupted another couple at Belton Bridge Park because it was a common meeting ground for lovebirds who wanted to spend some time together outside of their homes.

The interviews and investigation

Once Stacy got to the station, she started talking. She was asked to explain what they were doing at the remote park and she admitted that they did have problems in their marriage. She thought this would be the perfect time to add some flare to their relationship. Since Richard was a stay at home dad and she had difficult work hours, the two simply couldn't get any alone time to spend with each other. She was becoming desperate and unhappy.

She quickly admitted to having an affair to the shock of everyone who was present in the interrogation room. Her lover was a fellow co-worker from the hospital who was significantly younger than Richard. His name was Juan and he was a complete opposite of Stacy's husband. She needed intimacy and she fell in love with someone else who could give her everything she craved for. Stacy even took her lover to Las Vegas just a couple of weeks prior to the murder of her husband.

The detectives were interested in the affair and started asking questions related to the possibility that Stacy wanted to get out of her marriage with Richard in order to be with her new man. Stacy told them that she did think about leaving Richard but that no particular plans were made. She knew how much her children loved him and getting a divorce would probably break their hearts. They focused on Stacy's lover but she quickly debunked their claims by saying that he is not violent at all and that she cannot imagine him being involved with anything involving guns or shooting.

But Stacy did say that Juan knew about the rendezvous in the park so the police decided to call him up for an interview the next morning. Juan seemed oblivious to the events that took place last night and he told the detectives that Stacy claimed her relationship with Richard was open. This meant that each of them had someone on the side. Juan didn't seem to be bothered by this arrangement at all so the investigators started doubting their possible theory. Plus, Juan had a solid alibi for the time of the murder because he was in another city.

They were left without any solid lead in this case so it was time to look a bit further and include as much aid as possible. The park is a fairly isolated place but there was a nearby cell phone tower that covered the entire area. The investigators knew that if a call was placed from that location on the night of the murder, they would have the number listed. And it turned out that this was a crucial move made by the investigators because it would lead them in the right direction.

The list of calls was short because that cell tower is not in an urban area. The detectives used the contact information which was stored in both Stacy's and Richard's phones and they tried to find the match. Stacy's phone had the number that was called sometime around the murder. The contact info itself stood out because it said Mr. Results. The investigators were slightly confused because they had no idea who this person was. But calling him up would probably shed some light on the events that occurred on Valentine's Day.

The police quickly identified the mystery man who was present at the scene of the crime that night. His name was Reginald Coleman and he worked as a private fitness instructor in Atlanta. Coleman was born in Philadelphia but his criminal past led him to move out from his hometown and try to start over in another state. He was incarcerated in the past but managed to clean up his act. Coleman was doing fine financially and owned a fairly popular gym. As far as the local police force knew, he was staying away from any type of crime.

Todd Woodten who would become Coleman's attorney during the trial said the following on his client: "Reginald was a true survivor. He was street-savvy and always had a hustle going on. He did a lot of things for youth, trying to keep them off the street and keep them safe."

Once the police managed to attain the call records from Reginald Coleman's cell phone, they found the number he had called from the Belton Bridge Park. The investigators thought they would see Stacy Schoeck's digits but they were surprised with their discovery. Coleman called another woman - Lynitra Ross. The detectives then realized that the whole plot was more complicated that they initially assumed and that there are more players involved with the murder of Richard Schoeck. So how did all of them fit together?

After speaking to Coleman's friends, the police found out that Lynitra Ross was his ex-girlfriend who would often resurface in his life. But there was another detail that connected Lynitra to the murder – she worked at the same hospital as Stacy Schoeck and two of them were really good friends. Stacy was Lynitra's boss and a landlord. Since there was a third set of tire marks on the scene of the murder, the detectives quickly determined that the model did not fit the tires on Reginald's car. This did sidetrack them a bit but they were still determined to find out what really happened.

The investigators were certain that they did, in fact, have their suspect and that was Stacy Schoeck. However, they still had to connect the dots so they dug even further into the phone records of those three. There was a message exchange on the night prior to the murder of Richard Schoeck between the three parties. However, the most interesting clue was Stacy's bank account which clearly stated that she sent a total of $10,000 to Lynitra's account which she passed along to Reginald.

The arrests

Since the topic of the third vehicle was still the big unknown, the police started going through all cars which were somehow related to Stacy, Lynitra, and Reginald. And soon enough they were onto something. Stacy did have one car which she sold soon after the murder. It wasn't registered to her but she did use it often in order to drive her relatives or get them groceries. They were surprised to find out that Stacy put their vehicle on the market but she told them that they will get a newer model as a gift from her.

The police became very suspicious of this story so they tracked down the new owner and took a look at the tires as well as the insides of the car. And yes, the tire marks matched perfectly. Stacy Schoeck borrowed that car to Reginald Coleman on that fatal Valentine's Day. The evidence against Coleman was piling up and he was arrested on May 25th, 2010. But as soon as the interrogation started, he denied any involvement with Stacy Schoeck or the murder of her husband.

Lynitra Ross was arrested a couple of hours after Reginald but she also refused to provide the investigators with any useful information. It was time to pick up Stacy as well so the police arrived at the medical center she worked at and led her straight to the station. The investigators had plenty of circumstantial evidence to accuse her of the murder and they didn't have to wait for her accomplices to start talking about the crime. All three of them were in custody and it was time to face the justice for their actions.

Psychological assessment

Stacy Schoeck was put through a psychological assessment prior to the trial itself in order to determine if she had any underlying problems which were unknown to her or her family. The murder was well planned so she clearly wasn't distraught at the time which meant that Stacy knew exactly what she was doing when she asked her friend Lynitra to help her get rid of her husband.

The psychologists took a closer look at her prior relationships and marriages which ended in divorce. The reason for her unhappiness might lay in the fact that she lost her biological father when she was young and she was unable to connect to anyone. Not to forget that Stacy was also molested when she was just a child.

It was obvious that Stacy Schoeck was manipulative and knew how to get exactly what she wanted in every situation. Her intelligence was obviously high because she did put herself through school and successfully earned her degrees. However, her actions towards Richard Schoeck show that Stacy was also a sociopath because she hired a man to murder her husband and continued to live her life as nothing happened.

She mourned her husband publicly and got very emotional in front of her friends and family every time they saw her. The fact that she selected Valentine's Day as the date of the execution speaks volumes about her cold-heartedness towards Richard Schoeck.

The trials of Ross and Coleman

The first of three to stand a trial was Lynitra Ross. She entered the courtroom in May 2012 and was facing charges for a murder. After all, she was a co-conspirator who helped Stacy Schoeck find the hitman who would eventually pull the trigger and take Richard's life. Stacy was also present in the courtroom but she wasn't the accused in this situation. As a matter of fact, she testified on the side of the prosecution.

Stacy Schoeck was cooperating with the law enforcement and made a deal regarding her sentencing. She did everything to avoid the death penalty and was ready to talk about the murder of her husband. It was clear that her deeds were out in the open and she said the following as she took the stand: "I'm going to testify truthfully for Richard. It's all I can give his mom and his family and the children — all I can give them is the truth."

The jury then heard the story about the murder plot. Stacy Schoeck had the idea to take her husband's life in December 2009 after she noticed that her boys were acting strangely. They were getting into troubles and she started to suspect that they might be victims of molestation. She remembered how she behaved during the time she was assaulted as a child and found the connection. Of course, her first suspect was Richard because he was always with the boys.

Stacy also said: "I was just so fixated in my mind that Richard was doing something wrong that I said, 'I don't want the cops, I don't want a divorce, I want him dead.'" She then admitted to asking an unnamed man to help her kill her husband but he stopped returning her calls. Then she talked to her friend and co-worker Lynitra Ross and told her about her suspicions. Lynitra responded with the suggestion that they talk to her ex-boyfriend who would know what to do because he was "an experienced hitman".

After Lynitra Ross contacted Coleman, the two woman drove to his house and sat down with him in order to agree on some finer details regarding the hit. They talked and ate food from Zaxby's. Stacy suggested the park as the perfect place for executing her husband because he wouldn't suspect a thing. Reginald and Stacy agreed on the amount of money she would pay him for the murder, as well as on the vehicle he would take to the park. All three of them went to Belton Bridge Park so that Stacy could show him the exact place where her husband will be waiting.

Stacy noted in her testimony the following: "The only times I ever saw or spoke to Reginald Coleman was the day we had Zaxby's that afternoon and the following Saturday when we went up to Belton

Bridge. Everything else was done through Lynitra." She also added that she had given Lynitra the property she was renting to her as the payment for the help.

Lynitra's defense lawyers took the stand and told the jury that Stacy's testimony which involved the molestation claims was slightly off due to the fact that she admitted to having an affair in the first interview she gave after the murder. She didn't mention anything related to the possible sexual abuse of her children.

In August of 2012, Lynitra Ross was sentenced to life in prison. There would be no possibility of a parole either. Even though she didn't pull the trigger, she was the person who set up Stacy and Reginald to meet. Therefore, she was directly involved in the murder plot.

It was later determined that Richard Schoeck didn't have anything to do with child molestation but Stacy's plan was already completed and her husband was dead. The investigators took her claims seriously and talked to the middle boy who immediately said that he never accused Richard of anything. As a matter of fact, he never even talked to his mother about the alleged abuse. However, this didn't stop Stacy's attorneys from building their case around this.

Reginald Coleman's trial didn't last long because as soon as he appeared in front of the judge in November of 2012, he pleaded guilty to the murder of Richard Schoeck. He also faced charges for owning the firearm as a convicted felon. Stacy Schoeck was set to testify against him as well, which meant providing the courtroom with the full account of Reginald's actions.

Reginald Coleman agreed to kill Richard Schoeck after he heard the story of the alleged molestation directly from Stacy and Lynitra. Since he grew up in foster care, he often listened to the stories from his friends about their own abuse. Coleman thought that he could help the boys have a normal childhood by eliminating the threat from their life. He pleaded guilty in order to avoid the death penalty which was already on the table if he went on a trial. Coleman received the punishment of life in prison without the possibility of a parole and some additional years for the possession of the firearm.

Stacy Schoeck's trial

Once Ross and Coleman received their sentences, it was time for Stacy to appear in court for her own trial. The proceedings began in December of 2012 at Hall County Courtroom. Since Stacy cooperated with the prosecution in the trials of Coleman and Ross, the death penalty was off the table. Judge Jason Deal listened to the witnesses who described Richard Schoeck as a loving father and an exceptional friend who would never harm anyone. Stacy's defense attorneys once again repeated the story of the alleged abuse and claimed that her actions were severe because she wanted to protect her children from the aggressor.

When Stacy took the stand, she admitted to the crime and asked the judge to give her mercy. The defense told the courtroom about Stacy's own abuse and that she was acting erratically. However, the fact that the murder was planned months before it happened painted a picture of someone who wanted to eliminate her husband. Stacy had plenty of time to make sure that Richard was really the abuser and contact the law enforcement but she failed to do so.

Stacy's lawyers asked Judge Deal to consider giving Stacy a possibility of a parole and to keep in mind her troubled past. They also pointed out that Stacy was behaving well in prison and that she deserves a second chance. However, she received the punishment of life in prison without a chance to get out after serving thirty years which was the primary goal of her defense team.

Attorney Lee Darragh who led the prosecution said: "Judge Jason Deal appropriately recognized that Stacey Schoeck was the engine that put this train in motion, until the death of her husband. Without her involvement, this would not have occurred." The courtroom was filled with emotions because a large number of Richard's friends showed up for the hearing. One of the saddest moments was when Stacy's mother read a note which was written by her youngest boy which said: "I miss her every hour of every day, just like Daddy Richard."

Initially, Stacy Schoeck and Lynitra Ross were placed in two separate prisons in order to avoid any possible conflicts between the two but they were soon moved to the same facility – Pulaski State Prison. Stacy's family was left to wonder what was really the reason for this heinous crime because the exact motive was never uncovered. They got the custody of Stacy's three sons.

THE MURDER OF ASHLEY FALLIS

SARAH THOMPSON-CARLOS

What reason would a perfectly happy and healthy 28-year-old mother of two have for taking her own life? That is the question that seems to perpetually surround the case of Ashley Fallis, who was found dead of a bullet wound in the early morning hours of New Year's day in 2012. A beautiful young woman, Ashley was small and slight, with a bright smile and an attractive face. A photo of herself on her wedding days shows her kneeling it the grass with her children: her two daughters, Madelynn and Jolie, and her son, Blake. Her blond hair is elegantly pinned back off her face, and there's such joy on her face. It's hard to imagine that this young woman, so vibrantly fully of life, would take her own life and leave behind her three children, all under the age of 10 at the time of her death.

According to statistics gathered by the CDC, over half of American women who are killed have relations to intimate partner violence. After analyzing the murders of women in 18 different states, spanning across the years of 2003 to 2014, the CDC focused on exactly 10,018 different female deaths. Of all of those deaths, 55% of of them were related to intimate partner violence. Intimate partner violence can be described as family members, lovers, boyfriends, partners and spouses. That that definition in mind, even more chilling was the finding that in 93% of those cases, the perpetrator was a romantic partner, either current or former. It becomes even more unnerving to find out that 54% of those deaths were gun deaths.

It draws the question, with a statistical trend like this, is it possible that an otherwise happy woman, with her husband and children, would take her own life? Despite what her friends and family knew about her, was it possible that Ashley Fallis was hiding a secret depression so deep that she took a gun to herself to end it all?

Most people can't say that they married their high school sweetheart, but Ashley was one of the lucky few who could. Unfortunately, that relationship didn't last. They married soon after their high school graduation, and had two daughters: Madelynn and

Jolie. Despite the children, the marriage crumbled and fell apart, and the two divorced. It was in 2007 that Ashley met Tom Fallis, who would surely change her life. Tom Fallis was a responsible man, and he seemed to have his life together.

It was only one month into their new, budding relationship that Ashley fell pregnant once again. That was how Blake was brought into the family. Their son was what brought Ashley and Tom together, despite the shortness of their new relationship. It was only two weeks after Blake was born that Ashley and Tom decided to make their family official. Tom adopted Madelynn and Jolie, and they couple married.

As beautiful a story as it seems, Ashley's family felt as if the whole thing was moving quite quickly. After all, Ashley and Tom had only known one another for a month before she fell pregnant. Perhaps their relationship had grown closer throughout her pregnancy, and then after the birth of their son. Still, it was mostly unknown to Jenna Fox, Ashley's mother, and Joel Raguindin, Ashley's adoptive father. Ashley and her mother were extremely close, much more like friends than mother and daughter. Raguindin explained how they had tried to talk Ashley out of it before the wedding.

Tom Fallis seemed like an alright guy, at first. After all, he was ready to start a family. He seemed to have his life together. But, slowly, Ashley's family began to notice that there was something wrong with him. Tom Fallis had a problem with needing to be right all the time. He was aggressive, and seemed to always be ready to argue. Jenna Fox noticed it, and she didn't like it. Ashley's family was worried by the way Tom was acting, but there seemed to be nothing to draw the couple away from one another.

After the wedding, Ashley and Tom decided to settle down together with their three children in the small town of Evans, Colorado, just an hour outside of Denver. Tom took a jobs as a corrections officers at the Weld County Sheriff's Office, stationed at a local prison. Meanwhile, Ashley began working as a respiratory therapist. Those who knew Tom Fallis thought that he took the job as a corrections officer to feed his ego. After all, he was an aggressive person, according to Jenna Fox. He was also insecure. "He wanted total control of her," Jenna Fox told 48 Hours.

Jenna Fox also felt that she was a threat to Tom. After all, she was one of the only people that he could not isolate Ashley away from. The bond before mother and daughter was, seemingly, stronger than the bond between new husband and wife. The pressure to keep a balance between her new family with Tom and her relationship with her parents was put on Ashley. That pressure only increased when Blake, only just a toddler, was diagnosed with a brain condition. The condition was chronic, and would start to require almost all of Ashley's attention. Ashley was a doting mother, and did all that she could to give her son the attention and help that he required.

The constant attention that her son required, paired with the stress of Tom's increasingly controlling behavior was starting to take it's toll. Ashley was quite anxious, and overwhelmed with the situation as a whole. Still, Fox and Raguindin had never once suspected that Ashley was particularly depressed, nor did they suspect that she was suicidal. It just didn't seem like their daughter.

Still, Ashley and Tom's marriage was starting to feel the weight of that pressure. The two were considering a divorce, but apparently their relationship was slowly getting better as the holidays approached. The couple were planning a New Year's Eve party. And beyond that, they had received happy news. As the holidays closed in, Ashley had thought that she'd become pregnant again. They suspected that their family was about to grow even more.

That happiness only lasted so long. After she had gotten that positive pregnancy test, Ashley had stopped taking any medication just in case. After all, false positives happened all the time, and she wanted to make sure that whether the pregnancy was legitimate before she continued on. However, the day of their New Year's Eve party came and

Ashley began to bleed. Perhaps she had simply not been pregnant at all, or perhaps she was miscarrying. Whatever the cause of her bleeding, Ashley had been excited for the new baby. Learning that she was no longer pregnant caused her some significant sadness.

Despite learning that she wouldn't be a new mother once more, Ashley and Tom went forward with their New Year's Eve party all the same. After all, the invitations had been made, and the guests were on their way.

The part was a disaster. Jenna Fox describes the way that the tension between herself and her daughter's husband was becoming almost unbearable. Fox told 48 Hours that she "knew that Tom hated me". Despite the friction between mother-in-law and husband, the party was beginning to wind down without major incident - that is, until Tom Fallis went into a blinding rage because he had overheard Ashley's uncle offering her some marijuana. He began to swear, furious and loud. He told her that she didn't need to get high, even if she was still upset about the miscarriage. He told her, "It happened," and then told her that they were leaving, and to "Fuck everybody," and just let it go.

As Ashley's parents were leaving the party, they observed as Tom went into the bedroom, slamming the door behind him. Ashley walked them out, and they said their goodbyes at 12:04 am, after the New Year's ball had already dropped. Fox didn't observe anything out of the ordinary about her daughter. She didn't seem upset by Tom's behavior, after all. It wasn't out of place for Tom to act like this, and become enraged and swear. As Fox and Raguindin hugged their daughter and said their goodbyes on the front porch, they had no idea that this would be the last time that they saw their daughter alive.

Ashley isn't here any longer to tell us the rest of her story. What we know of that night is what Tom Fallis claims happened, and the autopsy reports, and the police records. As they guests filtered out of the house, they were among the last to see Ashley Fallis alive. When the last guest left and the door closed, no one but Ashley and Tom Fallis really know what happened that night that lead to the death of Ashley early in the hours of New Year's Day.

According to Tom Fallis, Ashley came into the bedroom in a defiant mood, and he said that she told him that if she wanted to get high, then she would get high. Tom told police that he told her to do whatever she wanted. Tom told the police that he had been in their closet, getting changed, when he heard the sound of her loading a gun across the room. Supposedly, it was the .9mm Taurus that Ashley kept under her mattress. As Tom walked out of the closet, he asked her what she was doing - and then, he heard the sound of a gunshot. Tom claims that he ran across the room to where Ashley was and held her head where the gunshot wound was, then grabbed the phone and dialed 911.

A recording of Tom Fallis' panicked 911 call plays Tom's voice, panicked and screaming: "My wife just shot herself in the head! Please help me! Please help me!" While the 911 operator tries to get his exact location and calm him down, Tom's voice comes through the call, tinny and screaming: "Ashley, no! Ashley, no!"

Finally, as the 911 operator tries to get more information, Tom can be heard shouting at his dying wife: "You are not leaving me! You are not leaving me! Stay right here!"

All in all, Ashley's family had only been gone for ten minutes. Ten minutes previous, Ashley had been on the porch, saying goodbye to all of her loved ones after celebrating the incoming of the new year. Her parents weren't even home, yet. They were still on the road when they saw the squad cars that were dispatched due to the call made by Tom.

At the hospital, Jenna Fox told 48 Hours that she knew, from the moment that she had seen her daughter lying in the hospital bed, that Tom Fallis had been involved. Perhaps it was a mother's intuition. Whatever the reason, Fox had no doubt that her daughter wouldn't have committed suicide. Even with the grief of her miscarriage hanging heavy over her that New Year's Eve, she was surrounded by her family and loved ones. Fox didn't believe for one second that suicide was an option for her daughter.

Ashley Fallis hadn't died immediately from that gunshot wound. She arrived at the hospital with severe trauma to the brain. But she wouldn't recover. The last time that her parents saw her alive and sentient was on the porch, ten minutes before she took a gunshot wound to the head.

But what happened? Tom's versions of events are clear. Ashley came into the bedroom, angry, and took a gun to her own head. Despite the fact that statistics put female suicides by firearm at only 31.2% (compared to male suicide by firearm at 56.4%), is it possible that Ashley had chosen such method? Women who commit suicide are often going to chose a less painful method, and one that would not leave behind such a mess. Pills and cutting of the wrists are much more popular methods when it comes to women who take their own life. But perhaps it was Ashley's grief that had driven her to take her own life with the gun she kept under her mattress.

Was it?

Despite the fact that Tom Fallis called in a suicide to 911, the police thought that it was important to question him about what happened. The police brought Tom Fallis into the station early on the morning of New Year's day, leaving his parents to watch his and Ashley's three small children. While Tom's frantic 911 call had seemed genuine, the police weren't all too sure. Neighbors had reported that they could hearing yelling and arguing coming from the couples house. Being questioned by Detective Rita Wolf, Tom was immediately put under scrutiny. The wound on Ashley's head was near the back. When told that her wound wasn't consistent with a suicide shot, Tom simply replied, "Bullshit! I didn't shoot my wife."

When investigators searched Tom's body, they found scratches on his chest, which he had said were from himself itching at his newly shaved chest. But that's not all investigators found. When they went into the Fallis' residence to take stock of the scene of the suicide, they discovered something strange. Tom's version of events had Ashley coming into the bedroom in an agitated state, then simply going across the room to retrieve her gun from under her mattress and shoot herself in the head. The state of the house, however, was inconsistent with that story.

Investigators found that pictures had been strewn from their place on the wall. It looked as if there had been a struggle. Not only that, but divorce papers had been found placed in a drawer. Tom Fallis had insisted that things had been going alright with him and Ashley, and that while they had been struggling before, things were moving in the right direction. The mere presence of divorce papers seemed to speak volumes, going against what Tom Fallis claimed was going on in his supposedly happy family.

At the hospital, Ashley Fallis had bruises on her legs. All of the evidence that investigators were digging up seemed to show that something else had gone down after all the guests had left the party - and that it wasn't suicide. Still, even after Tom Fallis was questioned for hours, he was released later that morning without charges being pressed against him.

Raguindin told 48 Hours that he and Fox were "shocked that they let him go." Even more shocking was what happened after that. Detective Wolf had told Tom Fallis that she didn't believe that Ashley could have inflicted that gunshot wound on herself. The position of the wound at the back of her head wasn't consistent with a suicide. Still, on January 5th, the coroner made an official ruling, and Ashley's death was listed as a suicide. Officially, the case was closed.

That seemed to be that. Ashley Fallis, wife, mother of three and devoted caretaker of her special needs son, was said to have taken her own life in the early morning hours of January 1st, ten minutes after waving goodbye to her family on the front porch after their New Year's Eve party.

The story for Tom Fallis, however, would go on. He packed up his children and moved them to Indiana, where he would attend graduate school. Despite the stress and strain of the relationship between Tom and Ashley's parents, they were determined to keep in contact with him for the sake of continuing a relationship with their grandchildren. After all, they were the only pieces of their daughter that they had left.

Life went on. For two years, Ashley's parents mourned their daughter's untimely death, and maintained a relationship with a man that they hated for the sake of their grandchildren. It seemed like no one else believed that Ashley wouldn't have taken her own life, and no one else believed that Tom Fallis was at fault. Until, one day, two years after Ashley's death, a man named Justin Joseph caught wind of the case. Joseph was a television news reporter with a source in law enforcement. Turns out, Ashley's parents weren't the only ones who were perturbed by the case.

Two years had passed, but Joseph took on investigating Ashley's story, anyway. Nothing seemed to sit right, and it was finally time to bring Ashley the justice that she deserved. Months were put into interviewing neighbors and friends who had already been cleared by the police, all of their statements taken and their concerns brushed off. In April of 2014, Joseph interviewed one of the Fallis' next door neighbors, Nick Glover, and found just what he needed to bust the case of Ashley's death wide open again.

Glover's versions of events differed from Tom Fallis'. According to Glover, he had heard Tom come out of the house, so he knelt down beneath the window sill to stay out of sight while he listened. Tom's parents were outside, and Glover could hear Tom saying, "Oh my god, I can't believe I did it." When his parents pressed him for more information, Glover heard Tom say: "I shot her." Of course, this wasn't the first time that Glover had told someone what had happened. In fact, the day that he was questioned by Evans Police, Glover told exactly the same thing to a Detective Michael Yates.

Glover's mother, Kathy Glover, had gotten a phone call that night from another neighbor by the name of Chelsey Arrigo. She told them to call the police, because she was sure that Tom Fallis had just shot his wife. Arrigo had heard Ashley yelling for Tom to get off of her, and the pop of the gun.

Everyone seemed to know what happened that night, and nothing was done. In fact, Detective Yates hadn't even written the report correctly. In his report of the incident that night, he quoted Arrigo as saying Ashley shot herself, not that Tom Fallis had shot her. Yates had also claimed that Glover had never told him about overhearing Tom admit to the murder of his wife. With contradicting statements, no one knew why a follow-up hadn't been given. Arrigo hadn't even been interviewed, despite knowing that Kathy had been in contact with her the night of Ashley's death. The case had been handled poorly from open to close, and no one seemed to know why.

Joseph found another person who had heard Tom Fallis admit the the murder of his wife: a sheriff's deputy who happened to be at the scene. It wasn't until two years later that he came forward to tell the investigators what he head heard. It's unclear as to why the case of Ashley Fallis wasn't treated as a homicide, or why no one seemed to take Glover seriously when he had told them what he heard, or why the sheriff's deputy said nothing to anyone until two years after the fact.

Was it a cover-up by the police? Or was it simply serious human error that caused the police not to go back and re-interview the people who had said they heard Tom Fallis admitting to murder? It seems hard to believe that the police would simply brush away Detective Wolf pointing out the position of the gunshot wound on Ashley's head, and two witnesses who had heard Tom Fallis saying clearly, "I shot her." One would want to hope that it was a serious error, and not the police deliberately looking the other way. There's no explanation for why Ashley Fallis' death was ruled a suicide, despite the evidence of a struggle in their house, and the witnesses that described Tom Fallis has raging and angry that night.

Whatever the reason that Ashley's case was closed, it was Justin Joseph that got it re-opened. His investigating opened up some serious questions about that night, and why the police had moved forward to rule her death a suicide. The case was reopened by a Evans, Colorado neighbor, Fort Collins, along with their much larger police force.

Tom Fallis had more information for the police, too. Two years after Ashley's death, Tom Fallis came forward during the new investigation with a suicide note that Ashley had supposedly written. There were several notes, one which read: "Dear Tom [...] I'm sorry for your pain. [...] I am a failure at everything." Of course, the timing of the suicide notes were suspicious. If Ashley had committed suicide, wouldn't the notes have shown up that first night?

Finally, it seemed like justice for Ashley Fallis was going to happen. In November of 2014, a grand jury made the decision to indict Tom Fallis for the murder of his wife. He was arrested in Indiana, and his children were put under the care of his parents. Tom Fallis had gotten away with putting his wife's supposed suicide in the past for almost three years. It wasn't until March of 2016 that Tom was finally put on trial.

The defense used Ashley's history of mental illness, anxiety, and the pain of her miscarriage to build a case against a dead woman. They claimed that it was Ashley who had shot herself in the middle of a crisis that early morning on New Year's Day. They pointed out that Ashley had been drinking at the party, and that there was even a history of suicide in her family: her uncle's mother and brother both died from suicide by gunshot. Was this just another suicide in a long line of tragedies? The defense seemed to think so.

Still, when Ashley's therapist took the stand, he made it clear that he did not consider Ashley a danger to herself or others. Still, Ashley was on medications from other doctors that she didn't tell her therapist. Defense used that against her, and in favor of Tom - saying it was entirely possible that Ashley Fallis could have written those suicide notes without telling her therapist.

When Ashley's parents were finally able to take the stand, they insisted that Ashley was fine throughout the night. Despite her miscarriage earlier in the day, Ashley was among family and friends. Her demeanor only changed when Tom became volatile. Jenna Fox described, once more, how Tom Fallis swore at them all and wished for them all to die before going into the bedroom and slamming the door.

Nick Glover also took the stand, repeating what he heard outside of his window that night. Tom Fallis' parents, however, denied that Tom had told them that he shot his wife. Kathy Glover also reiterated the phone call she got at one in the morning from Chelsey Arrigo. Unfortunately, when Arrigo took the stand, she couldn't remember making such a statement to Kathy Glover. All she remembered was hearing some arguing. Apparently, Arrigo was intoxicated because of her own New Year's celebration. Weld County Sheriff's Deputy, Chris Graves, was able to testify that he also heard with Nick Glover had heard that night, which was Tom Fallis admitting to shooting his wife. Still, he was questioned pretty hard after admitting that he should have come forward about it sooner than two years after the fact.

Forensic evidence didn't fair well in Ashley's favor, either. It was determined that the gunshot would very well could have been self inflicted. And yet, the prosecution called forward a forensic expert of their own, Jon Priest, who explained the exact opposite: no, Ashley's gunshot wound could not have been self inflicted.

There was so much testimony and evidence that the jury had to go through. The conflicting theories from the defense and the prosecution told two entirely different stories about what happened that night to Ashley Fallis. When the Jury retreated to deliberate the case and make their verdict, it didn't take them very long. In fact, the jury was only out for about three and a half hours. When they finally came back, Ashley's family could only wait with baited breath as the jury read out their decision.

Not guilty.

Tom Fallis was acquitted on the murder of his beloved wife, mother of his children. Ashley's family still holds their opinion that their daughter would never take her own life, and Justin Joseph maintains that the entire case of Ashley's death was handled poorly from start to finish. There was reasonable doubt that Ashley had killed herself that night, and there was no follow up done. Still, even after all the evidence was presented, the jury could not find Tom Fallis guilty. Whatever happened to Ashley Fallis that night will only ever be known by two people: Ashley and Tom.

THE MURDER OF BROOKE WILBERGER

83

OLIVIA WATSON

OLIVIA WATSON

Chapter 1

May 24, 2004 is a day many people in Corvallis, Oregon will never forget. It was the day a drunk man who was also high on crack set forth to destroy a life. Joel Courtney set out that morning in his 1997 green Dodge Caravan in search of a young, pretty co-ed to fulfill his dark fantasies. He cruised through the Oregon State University campus, searching, failing. But Courtney was persistent, and his wishes were soon fulfilled after he came across the Oak Park apartment complex a block down the road.

On the same morning, Brooke Wilberger woke up without any inclination that this might be her final day on Earth. She was newly home after finishing her first year of University, and was enjoying how sunny the spring had turned out to be. She headed over to the Oak Park apartment complex, which her sister managed, to help do some cleaning and basic repairs. Her sister needed help washing the lightposts out in the parking lot, so Wilberger grabbed some rags and a bucket of soapy water and got to work.

A few minutes into her work, Wilberger noticed a green van pull up. Inside, a man was waving an envelope at her, trying to get her attention. He looked like he needed help, so Wilberger approached. When the van pulled away seconds later, all that was left of Brooke was the soapy water and her now-broken flip flops.

It would be more than five years before Brooke Wilberger came home, but she would never come home alive. The story of her disappearance was a twisted tale full of hope, but it would only ever have a bittersweet ending.

Chapter 2

Brooke Wilberger was born in Fresno, California on February 20, 1985. She was the youngest of six. With three older sisters and two older brothers, she lived in a busy household, but it was a pleasant place to live. Her parents, Greg and Cammy Wilberger, were devout

Mormons, and raised their children to be the same. The family was incredibly close-knit.

Brooke Wilberger grew to be quite a beautiful, accomplished young woman. Besides boasting a strong set of mormon morals, she also excelled in school and had a lot of friends. The tall, thin blonde also received a lot of attention from the guys in her school, but she seldom dated.

The summer before Brooke began high school, the Wilberger family left California behind and moved North to Eugene, Oregon. Here, Brooke attended Elmira High School, and met her first serious boyfriend, Justin Blake. Blake also came from a mormon family, and was devoted to his religion, so the couple got along famously. They respected each other's minds, bodies, and faith.

The young couple graduated together in 2003, and while they were both dedicated to each other, they were on different paths towards the future. Wilberger wanted to go right to college so she could better equip herself with the knowledge she would need to turn around and better those in need around her. Blake was ready to jump into missionary work.

Wilberger was accepted into the Brigham Young University in Provo, Utah, and when she set off for her freshman year there, Blake set off for Venezuela to participate in a Mormon missionary campaign.

Although she was separated from her first love, Wilberger could not deny how happy she was at Brigham Young. The University was owned and operated by the Church of Jesus Christ of Latter Day Saints, and was the largest religious university in the country. She was immersed in her faith in new experiences and knowledge. She was actively participating in something much larger than herself, and she loved it.

Wilberger kept in constant contact with her family while away at University. She would often call and tell them about what she was learning, who she was meeting, and what she was doing. Her favorite topic of conversation, though, was always the inspiration her surroundings gave her to do better for the world. Although she was excited to see her family after the end of the year, she was in no rush to leave the busy, bustling campus for small-town Oregon.

After finishing her classes for the year, Brooke returned home to her family in late April of 2004. Her parents still lived in Eugene, but she wanted to maintain some of her freedom, so Brooke often stayed with her sister, Stephanie, who lived an hour outside of Eugene in an apartment complex she managed in Corvallis.

Her family were ecstatic to have her back home, close by, where they believed she would be safe.

Chapter 3

On May 24, 2004, Brooke had been home for about a month. She was staying with her sister in the Oak Park apartments, which were just down the road from Oregon State University, where summer classes were already in full swing.

That morning, a female student of Oregon State named Randy was walking through the Reser Stadium parking lot when she noticed a green van driving around her. When it pulled up next to her, the driver of the van got out and asked Randy for directions. The student had a bad feeling about the man, and when she looked in the back seat of the van she noticed a bunch of empty boxes and blankets. Before the man could get too close, Randy excused herself and hurried off to class.

Several minutes later, another student, Crystal, was approached by the same van in the same parking lot. Crystal did speak to the man, who again asked for directions, but the conversation was interrupted by an athletic's coach, who Randy had reported the earlier incident to. When confronted by the coach, the van's driver quickly jumped back into his vehicle and sped off of the campus.

While this was all happening, Brooke Wilberger was a block down the road from Reser Stadium at the Oak Park apartment complex. That morning she was planning on helping her sister Stephanie do some routine maintenance work on the complex. She decided to start with washing the lamp posts in the parking lot, so she grabbed a bucket, filled it with soapy water, and headed outside. Stephanie saw Brooke hard at work scrubbing the lamp posts at 10:00 a.m. It was the last time she ever saw her sister alive.

Shortly after 10:00 a.m., the same green van that had been causing havoc on the Oregon State campus pulled into the Oak Park apartment complex. The van pulled up to Brooke, blocking her view of the apartments. He began asking for directions, but when Brooke drew near, he pulled out a knife and forced the 19-year-old into the back seat of his van and sped away.

Five minutes down the road, the van pulled over and it's driver, Joel Courtney, got out and bound Wilberger's arms and legs with duct tape. He also covered her body with blankets he had stashed in the back seat. After this, he sped off towards a nearby area that was covered with heavy forestation.

Hours after Brooke was snatched from the apartment complex, her sister Stephanie realized that she hadn't seen or heard from her in a while. She decided to track her down to make sure she was okay, and began with the place she had last seen her—the complex's parking lot. When she got there she was surprised to see an almost empty parking lot, save for the cleaning supplies Brooke had been using and Brookes flip flop sandals, one of which was now broken.

Stephanie immediately ran inside and called police, who immediately launched a missing person's case despite their protocol stating they should wait 24-hours first. Brooke's broken flip flops at her last known location triggered enough of an alarm.

When detectives arrived at the Oak Park apartments, they quickly discovered that her truck, purse, phone, and wallet were all still at the apartments. If she had left the apartments by herself, she had done so without any identification, money, and shoes. It seemed unlikely that this would have been the case.

The search for Brooke began in the same way most crimes do—with the victim's significant other. In this case, Brooke's long-term boyfriend was quickly eliminated because he was over 4000 miles away doing missionary work in Venezuela. Brooke's family was also quickly ruled out.

During this process, the word of Brooke's disappearance quickly got out to the community, and a massive volunteer search was launched by the Wilberger's Mormon church. Within days of Brooke's disappearance, both Eugene and Corvallis were covered in missing posters detailing Brooke's physical appearance and last known location. Over 4000 acres of heavily-wooded area outside of Corvallis was searched for any signs of the missing girl over eleven days. None were found.

Police soon began to realize that the best chance they had of finding Wilberger would be to find the person who had taken her from the Oak Park apartments, so they quickly began to focus on the few early leads they had in the case.

The method in which Wilberger was abducted led police to believe that her abductor was a repeat offender. It's difficult to grab a grown woman off of the streets without anyone seeing or hearing anything. Police began looking through sex offender registries and crime logs to create a suspect pool, one that turned out to include over one thousand names, all of whom were interviewed.

One of the first people contacted by police was 45-year-old ex-con Lauren Hugo Krueger. He had been convicted in 1985 for attempted rape and had served time for the felony assault and kidnapping of a 23-year-old jogger. Krueger had also been questioned in relation to several reports of harassment and stalking. Most damningly, Krueger had also been spotted at a car dealership less than a block away from where Wilberger was abducted from. It was a promising start to the investigation.

Chapter 4

Many police officers in Corvallis believed they may have identified the man who abducted Brooke Wilberger on May 24, 2004, as being Lauren Krueger. He had committed several similar crimes in the past, making him a likely suspect. However, when he was interviewed, police discovered he had an airtight alibi for that afternoon, and he was eliminated in the case.

Shortly after Krueger was eliminated as a suspect, another man by the name of Sun Koo King was identified as a probably suspect. King was an Oregon State graduate who was unemployed and lived in the area. He had recently had a lot of trouble with the law for breaking and entering into Oregon State dorm rooms and stealing their occupants underwear.

Detectives searched King's home and found a startling collection of women's underwear, used tampons, and pubic hair. King also catalogued where he found each object of his collection, which allowed investigators to see that he had gotten most of the items from dorms at the University and from the laundry room at the Oak Park apartments, the same apartments Brooke Wilberger lived in with her sister.

Police were shocked by what they found at King's home, but what shocked them more was that there seemed to be no sign of Brooke Wilberger anywhere. Further, King passed a polygraph test and seemed to have an airtight alibi. Investigators were again forced to abandon the promising lead.

By October 2004, five months after Brooke's disappearance, police had a third strong suspect—Aeryn Evans. Evans had been arrested the month before for attacking a Oregon State student on campus. Evans' step sister called police after the incident suspecting that he may have been involved in Wilberger's disappearance too, but this was quickly discovered to be impossible by police.

Frustrated by having to eliminate three great suspects in a row, police decided they needed to take a different approach in the hunt for Wilberger's abductor. They decided to focus in on the one piece of evidence they had directly connected to the person who took Brooke—a green Dodge Caravan.

Police suspected that the green van was connected to Brooke's disappearance because of the two earlier reports from Randy and Crystal on the Oregon State campus, as well as from a tip call from a man who identified himself as Brian. Brian told police that he had seen a green van driving around the area Brooke was last seen. The driver was acting suspicious enough that the van had stood out to the man. The three incidents were too bizarre for police not to connect with Brooke's disappearance on the same day.

Both Randy and Crystal were interviewed by police, but neither were able to give a clear description of the van's driver. They had both been too spooked at the time. However, the coach that had intervened in Crystal's encounter with the van had gotten a good look at the van itself and was able to provide police with more details, including the fact that the van had had Minnesota license plates.

While police were now convinced that the van seen on the Oregon State University was the van used in Wilberger's abduction, they still had no idea where to find the van, and no idea who had been driving it. By November, 2004, six months after Brooke's abduction, investigators assigned to the case were still on square one. Little did they know though, that another crime was about to be committed in Albuquerque, New Mexico, and this crime would lead them right to Wilberger's killer.

Chapter 5

On November 29, 2004, a 22-year-old Russian exchange student, who goes by the pseudonym Natalie Kirov, left the daycare she worked at on the University of New Mexico campus for home. Minutes away from her doorstep, a car pulled up next to her and a man jumped out and told her to get into the car. Terrified, she complied.

The man held Kirov captive in his car at knifepoint as he drove off. When they got to a secluded area of a dead end road, the man pulled the car over and began to sexually assault the young woman, forcing her to remove her clothes in the process.

After sexually assaulting the Russian beauty, the man declared that he needed a drug fix, a "pick-me-up," and drove to a shady apartment complex to purchase some crack. He left Kirov in his car, bound up with her own shoelaces. While her captor was inside, Kirov managed to free her hands and unlock the car. She immediately ran into the street, despite being mostly naked, and flagged down a passing car.

Just as Kirov settles into the car she flagged down her captor emerged from the nearby apartment. After seeing how terrified Kirov became, her saviours quickly drove off in the opposite direction and brought her to the police station. She was finally safe.

Police immediately responded to Kirov's report by visiting the apartments her attacker stopped in to buy his drugs. They were able to find a lady willing to admit that a guy named Joel matching Kirov's description had stopped by earlier that night. Further, she knew where Joel lived.

Police immediately proceeded to the address given to them and immediately spotted the red car Kirov described parked in the lot outside. Police had just begun examining the vehicle when they were approached by a man who said he owned the car. Police asked him if his name was Joel, and he immediately responded yes. Police responded in turn by arresting him.

The Joel police now had in custody was Joel Courtney—a 38-year-old mechanic fisherman. Joel lived in Albuquerque with his wife and three children, but his marriage was incredibly unstable. Only a few weeks before this arrest, Courtney's wife had taken out a restraining order on him.

When police dug deeper into Courtney's past, they discovered that he had a long standing drug problem that they were able to trace back to his childhood in Beaverton, Oregon. Courtney had grown up an average, loving family, but his life began deteriorating after he started using drugs at the tender age of 11. By the age of 14, Courtney began repeatedly molesting his sister and cousins, and by the age of 19, he began experimenting with satanism, and was arrested several times for sexual assaults.

Now, many years later, he was back in custody for the sexual assault of Natalie Kirov, but it had been almost 20 years since he had been committed a crime, something Albuquerque detectives were skeptical of. They wondered if he had victimized any other women who crossed his path over the years, so they contacted authorities in Oregon, Courtney's home state, to ask if there were any unsolved crimes that matched Courtney's modis operandi. Almost immediately, Oregon police mentioned the disappearance of Brooke Wilberger six months ago, hoping to finally provide some answers to Wilberger's family and the surrounding communities.

Chapter 6

After having Joel Courtney brought to their attention, the Brooke Wilberger taskforce in Corvallis, Oregon decided to look further into Courtney's past to see if they could connect him to Wilberger's disappearance. They were quickly rewarded for this decision.

Investigators soon found out that Courtney and his wife had only recently moved to Albuquerque, New Mexico. Before that, the couple moved around Oregon frequently looking for cheap accommodations. At the time of Wilberger's disappearance, the couple were living with relatives in Portland, Oregon, an hour's drive away from Corvallis.

Further, investigators found that Courtney had been working for a janitorial company in Corvallis while he lived in Portland. He drove the company's 1997 green Dodge Caravan with Minnesota license plates to and from work each day.

Courtney's van was the exact van police had been trying to track down for the last several months. Armed with this knowledge, police managed to track down the vehicle, which was immediately brought to Portland to be searched for any forensic evidence that may have survived. Specifically, they were looking for any DNA evidence to compare to known samples of Brooke Wilberger and Joel Courtney himself.

While investigators waited for the DNA results to come back from the lab, they looked into Courtney's whereabouts the day Brooke Wilberger disappeared. They discovered that Joel Courtney had actually been expected in court to face a DUI charge that very day.

Police learned that on this day Courtney apparently made a call from Corvallis saying he would be late for his court time, but he never appeared. Police also learned that the next day, a disheveled Courtney had shown up at a family member's house 16-hours away from Corvallis. When asked why he was in such a state, Courtney came up with a story of how he ran into a gang of men in the woods who had captured a young woman and forced him to do terrible things he did not want to do. Amazingly, the family member chalked the unbelievable story to Courtney's chronic drug use, and never asked about it again.

On the one-year anniversary of Brooke Wilberger's disappearance, Corvallis investigators finally received the results of the forensic sweep of the green Dodge Caravan. It was worth the wait.

The evidence recovered from the van conclusively proved that not only had both Brooke Wilberger and Joel Courtney been in the green van, but Joel Courtney had been the person to place Wilberger there, and he likely knew where she was now. The final challenge investigators now had was getting Courtney to reveal this information so they could finally bring Brooke home.

Chapter 7

On August 2, 2005, Joel Courtney, who is preparing to go on trial for the kidnap and sexual assault of Natalie Kirov is served an arrest warrant for the kidnap and presumptive murder of Brooke Wilberger. Weeks later, the Kirov case is brought to trial, and faced with the indisputable evidence against him, Courtney pleaded guilty. He was given a sentence of 18 years in prison.

But Joel Courtney didn't have long to get settled in the New Mexico prison system. In April of 2008, he was extradited to Oregon in order to stand on trial for the charges laid against him in Brooke Wilberger's case.

When the trial began in Spring of 2009, the prosecutors in the case showed the court Joel Courtney's long standing history of sexual assaults against women, which dated back to his late teen years. They also presented a witness that had seen Courtney the night before Wilberger's abduction. This individual stated that they used to work together, and that they had spent the night of May 23, 2004, drinking and smoking crack together.

Although prosecutors had a large amount of evidence against Courtney, they were missing something very important, something desired not only by them but also by Wilberger's family and the entire community of Corvallis and Eugene—Brooke.

Up to this point, investigators had been unable to find any indication of Brooke's final resting place, and Courtney wasn't about to give this information up easily. The Wilberger family was all but begging the prosecutors and investigators working on Brooke's case to make a deal with Courtney so they could bring their daughter home and give her a peaceful burial.

The District Attorney eventually succumbed to the Wilbergers' wishes and presented a plea deal to Joel Courtney. The terms of the plea deal stated that Courtney needed to plead guilty to all charges against him and reveal the location of Brooke's remains. In exchange, Courtney would receive life in prison without parole.

Courtney rejected this initial offer, but quickly returned to the bargaining table. Courtney offered to plead guilty to the crime if he could be locked up in New Mexico near his family instead of in

Oregon. He also promised to reveal the location of Brooke Wilberger's remains. Courtney's counter-offer was accepted and signed.

To uphold his side of the plea deal, Joel Courtney drew a map to Brooke's burial site for investigators and walked them through the events of May 24, 2004. He told investigators the story of how he forced the young woman into his van and took her to some nearby woods to sexually assault her. After being raped, Wilberger became enraged, and tried to fight her way to freedom. Courtney responded by punching Wilberger until she fell unconscious before beating her to her certain death with a piece of wood he found nearby.

Based on this confession, and armed with Courtney's map, investigators drove 10 miles outside of Corvallis to a heavily wooded area known as the Coast Range. Their goal: to locate Brooke's remains.

After several days of searching, investigators were finally able to locate Brooke Wilberger's remains in a shallow grave next to a clearing of trees. Her grave was hidden beneath a mound of tree branches and leaves. For the Wilbergers, the news was bittersweet. They finally knew what happened to their daughter, and they finally could bring her home, but up until this point they had always maintained hope that when she came home she would still be alive.

Joel Courtney was formally sentenced to life in prison without parole two months later, and was brought back to a New Mexico prison where he prepared to spend the rest of his days. It was the end of a violent sexual predator's freedom, but most importantly, it was the end of the mystery that had plagued Oregon police and Brooke Wilberger's friends and family for years.

Brooke was finally home and at peace, and the world was a little safer now with Joel Courtney now behind bars. This is little solace to those who continue to miss Brooke Wilberger dearly, but having some answers is inarguably better than none. Those who knew Brooke in life remember her as the sweet, caring angel she was. She had a good soul in her heart and a good head on her shoulders and would have undoubtedly achieved great things in life.

Brooke's family still keep in contact with the investigators that dedicated their time to bringing Brooke home—they attend the officers' retirement parties and exchange the occasional email—a small token of the gratitude they will always hold.

THE MURDER OF CAROL TAGGART

OLIVIA WATSON

On Boxing Day of 2014, a young man living in Fife, Scotland walks into the local police station to inquire about his missing mother, Carol Taggart. The young man is her son, Ross. Carol Taggart has been missing for three days. Her family is desperately worried, apart from Ross, who is still going out clubbing and hitting the town using Carol's credit cards.

Then police find Carol's body, devastating her daughter Lorraine and partner Shaun.

Growing up, the Taggart family were incredibly close. The family comprised of four members, Carol, the mom, Shaun, the dad, and Ross and Lorraine, who were brother and sister.

Ross is four years older than Lorraine and had a different father, but that never mattered to them. The two were very close as children, and Ross always looked out for his sister. Both were loved and cared for by Shaun and Carol.

Lorraine, who was both Shaun and Carol's biological child, was very close with her father. She was a daddy's girl. Likewise, Ross was a momma's boy, and proud of it. Ross and Carol shared a very close relationship, but Shaun always considered Ross to be his son through and through, and to Ross, Shaun was always dad. The two shared many happy father-son memories. Shaun had taught Ross how to ride a bike when he was younger; he had been there to take the training wheels off. They were a typical family of four.

Carol and her son shared a special closeness. Although there was always enough love for Lorraine, there was no denying that Ross had always been the favorite when it came to Carol. There was always a little bit extra love for Ross.

In his mother's eyes, Ross could do no wrong. To her, he couldn't lie, he couldn't cheat. Her family described her as believing that the sun simply shone out of Ross's backside. He was the golden boy.

But in his teenage years, Ross went through some significant changes. As a child, he'd always been a loving, supportive brother and son. He was outgoing, loved to meet new people, and always seemed to be smiling. When he got older, he became very introverted.

As a young adult, Ross never said much. He wasn't a man of many words. When he was displeased, he wouldn't speak up. He would just give an unmistakable look, and his friends and family would instantly know.

For his family especially, this was frustrating. They couldn't get into his psyche, or figure out what he was thinking. They would ask him why he behaved certain ways, but they would never get clear answers from him. Most of the time, they wouldn't get answers at all. Ross would simply give them a blank stare and go to hide in his room, isolated from the family and the rest of the world.

Ross knew he didn't need to work hard to be loved by his family though. He knew he was the perfect child in his mother's eyes, he'd always known it, since the day he was born. The pair had had years together to bond before Shaun and Lorraine entered their lives. They had a mutual feeling that it had always been just the two of them.

Ross was well aware of this connection, and he used it to his advantage. He used his mother's affection against her often, emotionally manipulating her to get his way. To those around Ross and Carol, Ross's behavior showed him to be lazy, unfair, and rude. He was a user and a narcissist. But to Carol, he was none of these things. He needed her, he was her only son, and he relied on her for everything. Ross eloquently played on every emotion Carol had.

Ross was lazy in life and expected everything to land in his lap. He was brought up in a beautiful house, went on beautiful holidays, and had beautiful cars. He was used to getting everything he wanted, so he saw no point in trying to work for anything. That seemed to be his outlook on life—why try when you know it will be provided anyways.

Ross's laziness wasn't a product of his upbringing. Lorraine, Ross's sister, grew up with all the same luxuries as him, but as an adult, she worked hard to make her parents proud. She understood the privileges she had and used them to better her life and become independent. Ross was the opposite.

In the eyes of her father, Lorraine was a roaring success. She worked hard in school, achieved high grades, held down jobs, and went off to college to study dancing, which had been a lifelong passion for her. While this was happening, Ross was at home cruising through life, spending most of it alone in his room or with Carol.

Carol always saw the best in Ross. She saw Ross's laziness as a struggle. She worked hard to please him, to make him know that he was her priority. Ross knew this. He knew he could use those feelings to make his mom support him financially. More than that though, Ross understood that he could play up his role as the helpless son to draw Carol away from other people who saw him differently, especially their family.

Carol defended Ross to no end when others tried to make Carol see she was being taken advantage of, but that wasn't enough for Ross. He wanted to isolate her. He wanted to be her entire world so the money and affection would never stop.

Carol and Shaun had very different ideas of how to deal with Ross behavior as he aged. Shaun wanted to be hard on their son. He believed that Ross, who was now in his early 20's, was old enough to learn how to hold down a job and stand on his own two feet. He thought coddling Ross was holding him back from being an independent adult, but Carol wouldn't hear it. She believed that it would just take time for Ross to come out of his slump. He would grow into a responsible adult; he just wasn't ready yet.

Shaun and Carol began constantly arguing about what to do with Ross. He had begun driving a massive wedge in between his parents. For years the couple argued, unable to come to any resemblance of an agreement on how to deal with their overgrown child. While Shaun was still adamant that Ross needed to become more independent, Carol began to aggressively prioritize her son above all else, even going as far as telling Shaun that Ross came before everything, including Shaun.

After 19 years together, Shaun and Carol separated. It was becoming clear to both of them that they were no longer on the same page in life, and there was no end to their fighting in sight. Both Shaun and Lorraine blamed Ross entirely for the separation.

Shaun was heartbroken by the separation, but there didn't seem to be anything he could do. He couldn't sit back and watch the woman he loved get taken advantage of by her son, especially when he was expected to submit to Ross's wishes as well. Reluctantly, he decided to move out of the family's house.

Now, the Taggart household consisted of Carol, Ross, and Lorraine. While Lorraine was saddened by the departure of her father, Ross was elated. He loved being the man of the house. Lorraine was disturbed by the new dynamic that was developing at home and left as soon as she could. She later described the two years where it was just the three of them together as the longest two years of her life.

After her separation from Shaun, Carol began suffering from bouts of depression, so much so that she was unable to disguise her sadness from her children. In her vulnerable state, Carol was even less prepared to stand up against Ross, who began exploiting her even more.

It was around this time that Lorraine began to understand the kind of person her older brother had developed into. He wasn't a lazy boy with no ambition; he was a user. He was bleeding his mother dry. Lorraine tried to warn her mom that Ross was taking advantage of her, but par for the course, she wouldn't listen. Lorraine was terrified that Ross was going to turn against Carol one day and that Carol would be left with nothing.

Lorraine tried to get her mother help for her depression. The more depressed Carol got, the more dependent on Ross she became, and Lorraine could recognize that that was a recipe for disaster. She went to appointment after appointment with Carol and tried to get her enlisted in different facilities. But this didn't help, Carol's depression got progressively worse. She was lost.

Lorraine recalls feeling incredibly frustrated with her brother during this time. While she was doing everything she could to try and help her mom, he continued to prey on her weaknesses. And for whatever reason, Carol continued to rely on Ross more and more, ignoring Lorraine's pleas and attempts to get her help. Lorraine couldn't crack through the glass that separated herself from Ross and Carol's relationship. As hard as she tried, she was always on the outside looking in.

After years of this, Lorraine couldn't take it anymore. She relented to the fact that Ross was always going to come first in his mother's eyes, and that there was little she could do about this. All she could do was try to make her mother proud by succeeding in her own life, and it was time for Lorraine to focus on this. She couldn't keep fighting a losing battle, so she left home.

Finally, Ross had his mother all to himself. Although at this point in his life, Ross was in his mid-twenties, he had no serious relationships outside of his relationship with his mother. He had cycled through a series of girlfriends, but unsurprisingly, none of them stuck around for long.

Carol, in her depressed state, also had a hard time maintaining relationships outside of Ross. She had no interest in dating, as she still had a strong love for Shaun, and she had little motivation to make or maintain friendships.

Carol and Ross's relationship developed into a non-sexual partnership. The two began going on holidays alone together, and they began spending all their social time together, it was the kind of relationship you would expect to see between a husband and a wife—not a mother and a son.

The more time the pair spent together, the more fused their lives became. Carol was now fully dependant on her son emotionally, but

Ross was still only using his mother to make gains for his own life, and Carol was completely unable to see this for herself.

Although the family of four had been close when Lorraine and Ross were younger, there was now a clear divide. While Ross and Carol were perfectly happy in their closeness, both Lorraine and Shaun found it incredibly strange. And they were no longer alone. Many friends and family members of Carol began questioning Ross's motives. There were very few people outside of Carol that saw Ross as a good man. To most, he was a bad apple.

When Ross recognized that his mother had become fully dependent on him, he began to exert dominant control over her. He no longer felt the need to be sneaky in his manipulations; he was comfortable being outright aggressive with Carol. When she disagreed with Ross or said no to him, he would get angry and withdraw, knowing she would work hard to get back in his good books, giving him everything he had asked for initially and more.

Lorraine saw the shift in her brother's attitude towards their mom and grew increasingly concerned. He was becoming nasty. His tone when he argued with Carol was sharp, condescending, and cruel. It sent the message that he was going to get his way no matter what.

Even though Shaun had been driven out of the family home by Ross, he continued to see Carol. The pair began to grow closer again, and Shaun worked to pry Carol away from Ross just a little bit. For a while, it looked like it was working. Shaun and Carol had grown very close again, and Shaun asked to move back in, thinking they had finally found a way to mend their broken relationship. But things did not go as planned. Before Shaun could move back in, Carol told him that she'd have to ask Ross for permission.

This set Shaun off. Throughout their separation, Shaun had continued to help Carol financially support herself and their children, as her depression had been making it difficult for Carol to work consistently. Shaun helped pay the bills; Ross did not. And Shaun and

Carol were adults. He saw no reason why Ross had any say in the matter. Shaun never moved back into the family home.

On August 11, 2012, Lorraine married her husband on a beautiful sunny day. It was the happiest day of her life, and one of the last happy day the whole family would ever spend together. Shaun proudly walked Lorraine down the aisle, and Carol, elated to be the mother of such a beautiful bride, was too swept up in the magic of the moment to care about Ross's dislike of her re-budding relationship with Shaun. The family was able to celebrate together openly. After this day though, Ross began to isolate his mother from the rest of the family further, something they all thought was impossible. When Lorraine had her first child a year later, Carol wasn't allowed to visit and see her first grandchild for over six months.

In October of 2014, Carol took Ross on vacation to New York City for his thirtieth birthday. Most people at the age of thirty have moved out of their parents' home, have started a career, and possibly even a family. But Ross's life couldn't have been more of the opposite, and he was pleased as punch about that. After they returned from their trip, Carol continued to indulge her son, spending over £1,500 on Christmas presents to give to him before the day even arrived. Unbeknownst to her at the time, Carol would never see Christmas that year.

Out of the blue, on December 23, 2014, Ross Taggart called the Fife police to report Carol missing. He told the operator on the other end of the line that he had gotten into an argument with his mom and she had simply walked out of the house. Because she had been suffering from bouts of depression for years now, he was worried that she had taken the argument too much to heart and had gone and done something terrible.

Investigators charged with looking into Carol's disappearance had several concerns about the nature of this phone call. While Ross sounded confident on the phone, he didn't sound worried.

Additionally, he had made a point of getting information across that isn't common when people usually report family members as missing. He seemed to be trying to set up a specific scenario; it was suggestive and manipulative. Unfortunately for Ross, manipulating the police was not as easy as manipulating his mother. Investigators were wary of Ross from the moment he picked up the phone.

Lorraine had not spoken to Ross in a very long time when she got a missed call from him while out shopping with her husband. She was nervous about why he was calling, so her husband called him back on her behalf. That's when Ross told them the news—Carol was missing.

Initially, Lorraine wasn't too worried. She was hopeful that Carol had merely begun to see Ross for who he was and needed to take some space from him and therefore wasn't answering his calls. She figured she would call her mom later, and Carol would see that it was Lorraine and she would answer. By the end of the day, Lorraine had called her mother over ten times but had received no answer. That's when she began to feel an overwhelming sense of dread.

Lorraine thought of several possible scenarios of why Carol had run off and wasn't answering her calls, and they all seemed to revolve around Carol's relationship with Ross. The most likely, she thought, was that Ross had hit Carol, and Carol had gone into hiding to protect him. Despite how little she liked her brother, Lorraine still never expected the truth to be what it was.

In the days after he reported his mother missing, Ross was closely watched by the police. His movements and actions were caught on CCTV cameras and were being monitored. In the late hours of Christmas Eve, he was seen walking around the caravan park where his mother owned a holiday caravan. A few hours later he was seen withdrawing cash using his mother's card. Even later that same night, he was seen buying drinks at a nightclub, again on his mother's dime.

After Christmas Eve came and went without a word from Carol, Lorraine began to heavily doubt her brother's account of what had happened right before their mother went missing. On Christmas Day, she got a call from the police. They had found Carol's car with her purse, wallet, and phone inside. At that point, they knew something terrible had happened. They knew she was gone.

On December 26, three days after reporting his mother missing, Ross went into the local police station to check in on how the investigation was going. The visit was captured on camera and showed the true lack of emotion Ross was exhibiting during this time. This visit raised further red flags regarding Ross's involvement in Carol's disappearance. There was no recognition of sadness in Ross as he eagerly asked questions about what the police had found out so far. He wanted to know exactly what the police knew, which made them feel like he was trying to figure out something more specific—were they on to him.

Ross's actions after his mother disappeared were suspicious to everyone around him. While his sister Lorraine and father Shaun were at home crying their eyes out, calling people, and trying to wrap their brains around what was happening, Shaun was carrying out his life seemingly as normal. He continued to go out to clubs and use his mother's cards on a regular basis, even buying movie tickets to see *The Hunger Games* at the cinema. He sold Carol's expensive jewelry, justifying the act by saying he was entitled to her estate according to her will. He was not acting as if he'd just lost the person who meant everything to him just a week ago.

By January 1, 2015, Ross was the sole target of the investigation into Carol Taggart's disappearance. The rest of Carol's family had picked up on this, as he had quickly become a topic of interest when police questioned them. Initially, it was just about Ross's behavior in the days following Carol's disappearance, questions like why is he still going out clubbing? Does he have permission to use Carol's cards?

But as time passed, investigators got less subtle with their questions. Eventually, they got to the meat of their queries and asked

Lorraine and Shaun the same question separately: do you think Ross would do something to Carol? Their answer was the same—absolutely.

On January 11, 2015, the Taggart family received the news they had all been dreading: Carol's body had been found.

Carol's body was found stashed beneath a caravan in the same park as Carol's. It was the same place Ross had been seen on CCTV footage stalking around on Christmas Eve. Her body told a horrifying story to police, a story of brutal violence at the hands of someone with nothing but hate in their hearts. She had been battered to death and throttled. Her neck had been broken, and she was covered in bruises. The damage was so horrific that when Lorraine was brought in to identify the body, she was only shown her mother's wrist, which had a distinctive tattoo on it, although decomposition hadn't yet made her face unrecognizable.

To both police and the rest of the Taggart family, Ross was the prime suspect. Above all else, Lorraine was angered that even in death, Ross discarded their mother. She was left outside alone, where it was cold and wet. He didn't make a mistake. He did not feel guilty. He had left the only person in the world who loved him outside in the cold alone for over two weeks, and he didn't seem the least bit sorry.

Three days after police found Carol's body, Ross was formally arrested and charged with his mother's murder. Lorraine and Shaun felt relief for the first time in weeks when they heard the news. It was unfair to them that Ross was allowed to live freely after taking the life of their loved one. They hoped that at least they could now get some answers from Ross on how he was able to commit such a terrible act.

As well as being charged with murder, Ross was also charged with perverting the course of justice after lying to police and taking measures to prevent investigators from discovering what had happened to his mother.

During his trial, which took place in Edinburgh in November 2015, the severity of Ross's attack on his mother became clear to Shaun and Lorraine for the first time. He had beaten his mother with his fists so severely that he had partially broken her neck. He then strangled her so violently that her neck snapped the rest of the way. It wasn't a crime committed from a distance. It wasn't cold and calculated. It had been done with his own bare hands, face-to-face with the woman who raised him, while she screamed out in pain and fought for her life. It was a lengthy, sustained attack, after which he wrapped her body in a sheet, put her in the trunk of her own car, and drove her out to her caravan where she stayed for several days before he went back and buried her beneath a neighboring caravan.

The case against Ross was overwhelming. Everything pointed towards him. The prosecution had been able to assemble hours of suspicious activities captured by CCTV cameras along with 188 witnesses and experts. Including Ross, the defense only presented two.

Just when the family thought they had heard the worst though, the prosecution presented a surprise witness whose purpose was to demonstrate further the lack of remorse Ross had for what he had done.

The witness was a young woman, who neither Lorraine nor Shaun had ever seen before. They soon heard that she had been contacted by Ross through the online dating app Plenty of Fish the night that he had murdered Carol. He was using the app to look for casual sex just hours after dumping his mother's body, unbeknownst to the young woman. To prove that the young woman was telling the truth, prosecutors presented the GPS log from Carol's vehicle. Both the locations of Carol's caravan and the young woman's house appeared on the log in succession.

As well as condemning Ross beyond a reasonable doubt, this information also provided insight into Ross's mindset the night he killed his mother. He was not remorseful in the least. He had felt powerful, dominant, and wanted to continue the adrenaline high he got from committing murder. He wasn't a normal human being—he was a psychopathic narcissist.

Despite the overwhelming amount of evidence against him, Ross took the stand in his own defense and denied having anything to do with the disappearance or murder of his mother. He stuck to the story he told police over the phone when he first reported her missing—she had simply stormed off into the night after an argument. His family, watching from the court, recognized the blank look on his face he always wore when he lied.

The jury in the case took less than an hour to reach a unanimous verdict of guilty on all charges. Ross received a life sentence, which meant he would spend a minimum of 18 years in jail. To Lorraine and Shaun, this was barely justice. He was set to be released from prison at a younger age than Carol had been when she died.

Carol's memory lives on in the hearts of Shaun and Lorraine, but their hearts will be forever broken. Carol had so much love in her, and it was incredibly difficult to see her taken away from them by the person that she loved the most. Ross had been her golden boy, she had given him everything she had and more, and just as those around her feared, Ross took everything from Carol. He took her money, her love, and ultimately, her life.

THE MURDER OF DOMINIQUE DUNNE

ERICA THOMAS

Destined for stardom

In November 1959, film producer Dominick Dunne and actress Ellen (Lenny) Dunne welcomed a new baby to their growing family. Dominique Dunne was the couple's youngest of three children, and their only daughter. Dunne and her older brothers grew up surrounded by the arts – in addition to the influence of their parents, who were active in the California film industry, the children were frequently surrounded by celebrities of the 50s and 60s – close family friends who were often guests at the family home.

Dunne and her siblings grew up in a large house in Beverly Hills, but moved around fairly frequently as Dunne attended schools across the country – in Los Angeles, Connecticut, and Colorado. However, Dunne's childhood wasn't entirely carefree – when she was just eleven years old, Dunne's parents divorced. A few years later, in 1975, her mother was diagnosed with multiple sclerosis.

Still, Dunne pursued her education. After her graduation in 1977, Dunne studied art and Italian in Florence, at the Michelangelo School and at the British Institute. When she returned to California, she worked briefly as a receptionist and translator for Los Angeles' Italian Trade Commission before venturing back to Ft. Collins to study acting at the Colorado State University.

Her studies in Colorado were short-lived, however, and Dunne left after only one year to start auditioning back in California. Just a few weeks later, she was offered her very first film role. Dunne's acting career took off quite quickly – in her first three years, Dunne appeared as a guest on many well-known television shows, including *Family*, *CHiPs*, and *Fame*. And after taking on roles in four made-for-TV movies, Dunne made her cinematic debut as Dana Freeling in the movie "Poltergeist."

"One day, she decided to become an actress and the next week she was on a back lot making a movie, and that from then on she never stopped," said Dunne's father Dominick in a piece he wrote for Vanity

Fair in March 1984. "She loved being an actress and was passionate about her career."

"At ease in a sophisticated world."

To her friends and family, Dunne was known as a friendly, kind person. Despite having grown up with wealth and fame, Dunne's father described her as "totally at ease in a sophisticated world without being sophisticated herself." Indeed, Dunne dressed in casual clothes, preferring jeans and t-shirts to the upscale fashions her peers sported – and drove a blue Volkswagen Bug convertible.

Dunne loved cooking, traveling, baseball, and languages – particularly Italian, which she continued to speak quite fluently. She also loved animals, and had a soft spot for unwanted strays. Dunne adopted a cat with a lobotomy, a large dog with stunted legs, a snake, and a rabbit, among many other cats and dogs.

Even before her role in "Poltergeist," Dunne was a firm believer in supernatural phenomena, and friends say she was strictly superstitious.

Instant attraction

Dunne met John Thomas Sweeney in 1981, when she was twenty-two and he was twenty-five. Sweeney worked as a chef at Los Angeles' trendy "Ma Maison" restaurant, and Dunne was immediately drawn to him. After their initial introduction at a party that autumn, the pair quickly fell into a romantic relationship – and moved in together only a few weeks later, into a rental house in West-Hollywood.

However, their passion soon resulted in the first of many quarrels between the couple. Dunne was, by that point, well-known in Hollywood – a popular girl with many friends. Sweeney, on the other hand, had grown up poor in Pennsylvania, the product of a troubled family life. Despite Dunne's attempts to include him in her world, Sweeney felt like an outsider and was ashamed of his uncultured family history.

While Dunne had grown up with a loving family that respected and addressed emotional issues, Sweeney was raised in a coal town with an alcoholic father who, his mother claimed, often dealt with his frustrations by beating her – often in front of their children. By the time he was fourteen years old, his parents had divorced, and his father had developed epilepsy.

"Bitterly ashamed of his family and filled with a sense of worthlessness because he was a member of it, (Sweeney) longed to escape into a larger and more exciting life," read an article published in *People* magazine in 1983.

Sweeney's desire for a better life led him to pursue a culinary arts diploma from a local community college. At the age of twenty, he crossed the country to California, where he landed a job working at a restaurant called "Picolo's." Only one year later, he started as a chef's apprentice at "Ma Maison."

He was a talented, ambitious chef – and was willing to put in the work to achieve his career goals. After two years of double shifts, Sweeney was given a leave of absence to spend a year working on the French Riviera before returning to "Ma Maison" – where he worked as chef Wolfgang Puck's chief assistant.

His position at the glamorous restaurant gave him an opportunity to get a first-hand look at the elegant world he so desperately wanted to be a part of. And, after meeting Dunne, he finally felt like he would be able to access it. However, along with his excitement at being with a talented Hollywood actress, there was fear and insecurity – and the lasting sense of worthlessness he felt as a result of his troubled family life.

His jealousy started to take hold of the relationship. His interactions with Dunne grew more patronizing and dominating, and he began showing up on sets where Dunne was working to intimidate her male colleagues. Eventually, even that wasn't enough – Sweeney started to come to Dunne's rehearsals and even her acting classes.

It seemed Dunne couldn't do anything on her own without having to first discuss it with her boyfriend, which usually resulted in an argument that Dunne would never win. The more Dunne resisted Sweeney's possessiveness and jealousy, the more frightened he would be that she would ultimately reject him. Often, this fear would become anger.

"Alex said he was scary."

Dunne had introduced Sweeney to her family during the summer of 1982, flying the two of them out to New York where most of her family lived. According Dominick's article in Vanity Fair, Dunne's brother Alex was the only one who had "voiced his dislike" of her new boyfriend.

"Although I could see that Sweeney was excessively devoted to her, there was something off-putting about him," Dominick said.

The first night, Alex told his father about an incident that had happened after Dominick had left the restaurant. Dunne had been recognized by a man in the bar, who called out her iconic line from the film "Poltergeist." According to Alex, "there was no flirtation," just an excited, if slightly tipsy, fan.

"When Sweeney returned to the table and saw the man talking to (Dunne), he became enraged. He picked up the man and shook him," stated Dominick. "Alex said that Sweeney's reaction was out of all proportion to the incident going on. Alex said he was scary."

The next day, Dominick was to meet Dunne and Sweeney for lunch. Although he said he arrived at the restaurant late, the couple still wasn't there – and Dominick was already on his second bottle of Perrier by the time his daughter showed up with her boyfriend.

"I was immediately aware that she had been crying, and that there was tension between them," Dominick said. "The lunch was not a success. I found Sweeney ill at ease, nervous, difficult to talk to. It occurred to me that (Dunne) might have difficulty extricating herself from such a person, but I did not pursue the thought."

Getting physical

As the couple began fighting more and more, Sweeney's reactions frequently turned violent. On August 27, 1982, Sweeney reportedly tore out handfuls of Dunne's hair after grabbing it and using it to knock her head repeatedly against the floor. Dunne managed to get away from Sweeney and fled to her mother Lenny's house, with Sweeney following close behind. While Dunne's mother refused him entry and even threatened to call the police, it was only a few days before Dunne forgave her boyfriend and returned to their home.

Despite Dunne's forgiveness, Sweeney attacked her again not even a month later. On September 26, during another argument, Sweeney grabbed Dunne by the neck and pushed her to the floor before he started to choke her. Luckily, a friend heard the loud gagging noises coming from the next room – "it was the worst sound I had ever heard" – and came in to break up the fight.

"He tried to kill me!" Dunne cried out. Sweeney denied her accusation, insisting that Dunne come back to bed. Instead, she went into the bathroom, where she escaped out a window to spend the night with a friend.

The next day, Dunne showed up at the set of *Hill Street Blues*, where she was to guest star as an abuse victim for an episode of the show. According to accounts from cast and crew on the set, the bruises on Dunne's face and neck were "realistic" enough that she hardly needed any make-up for her role.

Dunne spent the following days in hiding, trying to avoid the abusive, angry boyfriend who was searching for her. Eventually, she contacted him to end the relationship – and to demand he leave the home they rented together so she could live there alone. Still, knowing how unpredictably angry and violent Sweeney could be, Dunne changed the locks of the house before moving back in without him.

The final battle

That autumn, Dunne had taken on a new role – playing Robin Maxwell for the three-episode science fiction miniseries *V*. She'd completed filming the scenes for the first episode and was nearly finished with the second episode on October 30, when she invited her co-star David Packer to rehearse scenes together at her home.

The pair were hard at work when Sweeney called Dunne at around 8:30 p.m. – and then showed up at the house only ten minutes later. Dunne answered the door with the chain fastened, but Sweeney demanded she come out and speak with him. Packer asked if he should leave, sensing Dunne's discomfort with the situation, but she said she wanted him to stay while she stepped outside to deal with her ex-boyfriend.

Out on the driveway, an argument broke out. Sweeney was pleading with Dunne to forgive him and take him back, but Dunne refused. She'd reached her limit and was no longer willing to tolerate Sweeney's anger and violence. Like he'd done before, Sweeney suddenly reached out and grabbed her firmly by the neck, dragging her up along the driveway into the next-door neighbour's back yard.

Dunne was no match for Sweeney – the petite actress was a mere 5'1" and 112 pounds. Sweeney, 6'1" and close to 200 pounds, held her down and began to strangle her. She was unable to fight him off, and eventually fell unconscious.

Meanwhile, Packer watched the confrontation with growing fear – he could see Sweeney's obvious rage and jealousy. When he heard screams followed by a thud, he called the police, only to be informed that the location was outside of the department's jurisdiction. After hanging up with the officer, Packer called a friend and left a message on his answering machine explaining that if he was found dead, John Sweeney should be held responsible.

Eventually, Packer went outside to check on Dunne, and found her lying on the driveway with Sweeney crouched next to her. Sweeney asked Dunne to call the police, and this time, they said they would send an officer. When the police arrived and found Dunne still unconscious, they called an ambulance, which arrived only five minutes later.

Brain-dead

On the way to the nearby Cedars Sinai Hospital, Dunne's heart came to a full stop, but doctors were able to restart it once the ambulance arrived. However, examinations showed that Dunne had sustained extensive damage from the anoxaemia during her strangulation – and that although her heart had been restarted, there was no way for doctors to reverse the death of her brain.

"There were tubes in her everywhere, and the life-support system caused her to breathe in and out with a grotesque jerking movement that seemed a parody of life," Dominick recalled. "Her eyes were open, massively enlarged, staring lifelessly up at the ceiling. Her beautiful hair had been shaved off. A large bolt had been screwed into her skull to relieve the pressure on her brain. Her neck was purpled and swollen; vividly visible on it were the marks of the massive hands of the man who had strangled her.

It was nearly impossible to look at her, but also impossible to look away."

The hospital's staff did everything they could for Dunne, and after five days, her parents made the decision to remove her from the life-support systems that were keeping her alive. Dunne died instantly, and her heart and kidneys were donated to the hospital to be used for transplants.

Dunne's tragic death was a shock to the entire Hollywood community, particularly for Dunne's extensive network of family and friends. Hundreds of people attended Dunne's funeral, held on November 6 at the catholic Church of the Good Shepherd in Beverly Hills – the same church where Dunne had been baptized 22 years earlier. Her body was laid to rest near Los Angeles, at the Westwood Memorial Park.

"An act of passion and despair."

"If (Dunne) had been killed in an automobile accident, horrible as that would have been, at least it would have been over and mourning could have begun," Dominick said. "A murder is an ongoing event until the day of the sentencing, and mourning has to be postponed."

Sweeney was charged with Dunne's murder, and the case finally went to trial at the court in Santa Monica in early August, 1983. A *People* magazine article from October 1983 described Sweeney as a "young man in a black suit" seated at a long table, his face "white as an egg" and his large, pale hands "folded meekly" over a Bible.

"It is the fashion among the criminal fraternity to find God, and Sweeney, the killer, was no exception," Dominick remembered. "The Bible was a prop; Sweeney never read it, he just rested his folded hands on it. He also wept regularly. One day, the court had to be recessed because he claimed the other prisoners had been harassing before he entered, and he needed time to cry in private.

"I could not believe that the jurors would buy such a performance."

But Sweeney painted a very different picture in the courtroom than the true colors he'd shown to Dunne's family and friends. According to Sweeney's testimony, Dunne "provoked" the violent struggle that resulted in her death, because she had previously agreed to reconcile and had then refused to take Sweeney back. Sweeney said he "just exploded and lunged toward her" after she told him she'd been lying when she said she would live with him again.

He added that he "had no memory" of the event, only that he found himself next to Dunne's unconscious body, with his hands pressed around her neck. According to Sweeney, he tried to resuscitate her, and when that didn't work, he ran into the house and swallowed two bottles of pills – attempting suicide due to his panic and regret at what he had done.

Sweeney's lawyer Michael Adelson added that Dunne was a "snob," who was constantly telling Sweeney how he was beneath her. Sweeney's account of their relationship presented Dunne as two-faced and heartless, and he said she even told him that she had been leading him on.

Dominick even recalled receiving a phone call from the prosecutor for the case, district attorney Steven Barshop, in July, shortly before the trial was set to begin. Barshop explained that Adelson had requested that Lenny not be allowed in the courtroom – Adelson felt the presence of the victim's mother, confined to a wheelchair, would create "undue sympathy for her that would be prejudicial to Sweeney."

The "accident" was a "tragedy," Adelson argued, "not a real crime – an action of passion and despair."

However, no evidence could be found to back up Sweeney's story, and investigators were reluctant to believe him. There was nothing to support Sweeney's claim that he'd attempted to commit suicide, and even during his initial interrogation, Sweeney seemed to show little remorse for his part in Dunne's death.

In fact, the police officers who arrested him testified that Sweeney had seemed "quite calm and collected," and more concerned about what would happen to him than what had happened to Dunne – only about an hour and a half after he'd been arrested.

"I fucked up, I can't believe I did something that will put me behind bars forever," Sweeney reportedly told police when he was brought down to the station. "Man, I blew it. I killed her. I didn't think I choked her that hard. I just kept on choking her. I just lost my temper and blew it again."

When one of the officers made a comment about how well Dunne had been doing with her acting career, Sweeney retorted, "well, I was doing quite well in *my* career. I'm quite proud of what I've done."

Upon further investigation, it was revealed that Sweeney had obviously strangled Dunne for about five minutes – at least four minutes, according to the medical examiner. According to police, this makes Sweeney's story fairly improbable. Not only would Sweeney have had enough time to realize what he was doing while he was choking his ex-girlfriend, he would have had the opportunity to regain control and let Dunne live.

During the trial, Dominick remembers Barshop holding up a hand to the jury, silencing the room for a four-minute period – "how long it took for Dominique Dunne to die," Barshop said, in his opening statement.

"It was horrifying," Dominick said. "I had never allowed myself to think how long she had struggled in his hands, thrashing for life. A gunshot or a knife stab is over in an instant; strangulation is an eternity."

Barshop also brought forward testimony from one of Sweeney's previous girlfriends – a secretary named Lillian Pierce, who'd also lived with Sweeney. During their relationship, which lasted from 1977 to 1980, he'd abused her on at least ten different occasions – resulting in two separate hospital visits, one for a perforated eardrum and collapsed lung, and a second time with a broken nose.

"Later, we heard that (Pierce) had sat in a car outside the church at (Dunne's) funeral and cried," Dominick said, "feeling too guilty to go inside."

The testimony proved that unlike what Sweeney's lawyer had argued, this was not a unique crime of passion, but rather a pattern of abusive behaviour toward women. Still, Sweeney's lawyer was able to convince the judge that the testimony was prejudicial, and had it excluded from the trial.

"Her account of her relationship with John Sweeney was so shocking that it should have put to rest forever the defense stand that the strangulation death of Dominique Dunne at the hands of John Sweeney was an isolated incident," wrote Dominick. "He was, it became perfectly apparent, a classic abuser of women – and his weapon was his hands."

As he questioned Pierce, without the jury present, Adelson inquired about a specific discussion the witness had had with himself and another lawyer on November 3, 1982 – the day before Dunne was officially removed from life-support and pronounced legally dead.

"Even while (Dunne) lay dying, efforts were being made to free her killer by men who knew very well that this was not his first display of violence," Dominick said. "I felt hatred for Michael Adelson. His object was to win; nothing else mattered."

Testimonies from Dunne's friends and co-workers were also ruled out after Sweeney's lawyer argued that they were nothing but hearsay. These statements explained that Dunne was not remotely interested in a reconciliation with Sweeney – in fact, she'd spent the final five weeks of her life in "permanent fear" of her abusive ex-boyfriend.

Even without this important evidence, the prosecution still sought a second-degree murder conviction, with a minimum sentence of fifteen years.

The jury did get to hear a letter found by Dunne's friends, addressed to Sweeney but obviously never sent to him. The letter detailed Dunne's frustrations at the control Sweeney attempted to hold over her, and her desire to end the relationship.

"You do not love me. You are obsessed with me. The person you think you love is not me at all. It is someone you have made up in your head," Dunne said in her letter. "I'm the person who makes you angry, who you fight with sometimes. I think we only fight when images of me fade away and you are faced with the real me.

"The whole thing has made me realize how scared I am of you, and I don't mean just physically. I'm afraid of the next time you are going to have another mood swing. When we are good, we are great. But when we are bad, we are horrendous. The bad outweighs the good."

An unsatisfying result

The trial wrapped up at the end of September, and the jury found Sweeney guilty of voluntary manslaughter – to the shock of Dunne's family and friends. "The law protected him," the jury said, but several members later admitted that had they known about Sweeney's history of violence and abuse, they would have found him guilty of the second-degree murder charge.

"I guess there is never any real satisfaction that the legal system can give, but this – the outcome – was such a blow, such a slap in the face to our family and to (Dunne's) memory," said Dunne's older brother Griffin. "They literally got away with murder... the bitterness of that will never leave."

Even Superior Court Judge Burton S. Katz, who presided over the trial, felt the system failed to provide justice for Dunne's tragic murder. Barshop stated that this failure has allowed a "time bomb" to return to the streets, where he could potentially abuse again, and blames Katz for the many rulings he made that prohibited the jury from hearing important, relevant evidence.

However, Katz argued that he had no choice but to rule the way he had – but admitted that some of the more controversial rulings during the trial "pained" him. Shortly after Sweeney's trial, Katz moved to the Juvenile Court in Sylmar.

"Nothing is more difficult than rendering a decision based upon a law with which you disagree," Katz said. "Unfortunately, following the letter of the law sometimes doesn't permit one to pursue the ultimate goal of justice."

Sweeney ended up with a sentence of only six and a half years in prison, the maximum sentence imposed for convictions of voluntary manslaughter. Instead of the fifteen years the prosecution had hoped for, Sweeney was released from a medium-security state prison after spending three years, seven months, and twenty-seven days in custody.

"Three and a half years for a life is certainly not justice," Katz said. "If I could have given him 25 (years), I would have given him 25. If I could have given him life, I would have given him life... I agree with everyone that based on his past record of violence... he is dangerous to any woman."

Soon after his release from prison, Sweeney found another high-paying job as a head chef at a chic restaurant in Santa Monica called "The Chronicle." The new position didn't last long, though -

Sweeney was fired after Dunne's family and friends descended on the restaurant with handbills that were distributed to guests and passers-by.

"The hands that prepared your food strangled Dominique Dunne on October 30, 1982," the handbills read.

Sweeney left Los Angeles for Seattle in 1989, and changed his name to John Maura. According to some sources, he is currently employed there as an executive chef for a chain restaurant.

"This guy gets to be reinstated as the head chef in a restaurant as if nothing ever happened," said Dunne's older brother, actor Griffin Dunne. "If she had lived, she'd be an actress everyone in the world would know... he's a murderer; he's murdered and I think he will do it again."

Another friend of the family echoed these thoughts, adding that "the verdict almost says it's okay to kill the one you love."

THE MURDER OF FAITH HEDGEPETH

JESSI DAVIS

Happy-go-lucky

In 1982, Connie Hedgepeth had her hands full with two teenage daughters and a husband who was addicted to drugs. Her marriage was struggling when she took a pregnancy test, hoping the result would be negative. It wasn't. Her youngest daughter was born eight months later, and Connie named her Faith.

"I felt like it was my faith in God that helped me through that situation," she said. "My faith helped me to continue to work and to do what I needed to do for my children."

Still, Connie divorced her husband when Faith was still young. Struggling to stay afloat, Connie turned to her oldest daughter, Rolanda, for support. Despite an almost 18-year age difference, Rolanda and Faith developed a strong bond – "part mother-daughter, part sister," Rolanda explained.

"We were always close. I was kind of like a second mom, but there was that sister bond, too," she said.

Rolanda's daughter Alexis was born on Faith's first birthday, and the two girls grew up together in rural North Carolina. Her upbringing was difficult, but Faith's positive attitude and eagerness to contribute propelled her through her schooling. She was an honor student, a cheerleader, and a regular volunteer for many other clubs and organizations.

"She always had this energy about her," Rolanda recalled. "She was really happy-go-lucky."

Faith's father had dropped out of college to raise his family, and Faith intended to pick up where her dad had left off. She earned a Gates Millennium Scholarship to the University of North Carolina at Chapel Hill – the very school her father had been attending. Poised to be the very first college graduate in her family, Faith had plans to become a pediatrician or a teacher once she completed her education.

Instead, the Native American biology major never made it to her 20th birthday. Police records reveal that Faith was last seen alive at approximately 3 a.m. on September 7, 2012, when she and her roommate Karena Rosario came home after an evening partying at a local nightclub.

The Thrill of a lifetime

The night before she was murdered, Faith had been studying with Karena at the Davis Library, on the university campus. At around 8 or 8:30 p.m., Faith took a break from her studies to send a text to her father – "Hey Daddy, I love you," the message read. She also texted her niece, reminding her to register to vote in the upcoming election.

At around midnight, the girls left the library and stopped back at their apartment before heading out at approximately 1 a.m. to arrive at a nightclub called The Thrill.

Just after 2:30 a.m., the girls left the bar. Karena was feeling sick after having had too much to drink, and wanted to go home. Faith helped Karena get into bed, and then fell asleep herself. However, a text message from Faith's phone was received at 3:40 a.m. by Brandon Edwards, Karena's ex-boyfriend.

"Hey b. can you come over here please," the message read. "Karena needs you more aha. You know. Please let her know you care."

A few minutes later, another text comes through that simply says, "than." It is suspected that the message was intended to fix a typo in the original message, correcting it to say "Karena needs you more *than* you know." Brandon didn't reply until the next day, when Faith's phone received a text at 4:16 p.m. that read, "Who is this?"

At around 4:30 a.m., Karena left the apartment to go over to a friend's house – and claims that she did see Faith asleep at that time. When she returned at around 11 a.m., however, she found her roommate's body in her room, in her bed, "covered by a blanket on top of her slightly askew mattress with large amounts of blood."

At 11:01 a.m., a 911 call came from the house.

Faith was unconscious and cold, Karena told the dispatcher who took the call, and there was "blood everywhere." She said she thought there may have been an altercation, explaining to the dispatcher that "there were items in the room that were not hers and that it looked like someone else had been there."

Police responded immediately, securing the scene at the girls' apartment complex and collecting evidence. They found Faith's body "positioned on the floor, leaning against the bed, with her shirt pulled up and no clothes from the waist down."

Medical examiners concluded that the cause of death was blunt force trauma, based on the severe beating Faith had endured. When the autopsy report was unsealed nearly two years after the killing, it was revealed that she also had bruises and cuts all over her arms and legs, as well as blood underneath her fingernails.

"It's very, very hard, learning of how Faith died," said Rolanda. "She was beaten, she was bludgeoned to death. A lot of people don't understand what that means, but it was really bad."

A rape kit had also been performed, indicating the presence of semen – with DNA that matched other DNA that police had recovered at the scene. Law enforcement officials have not confirmed whether the sexual activity was consensual or forced.

Searching for suspects

In the years since Faith's death, multiple search warrants have been executed – as well as numerous court orders for things like cell phones, computers, and even social media accounts. DNA testing has also been carried out on many of men that interacted with Karena and Faith while they were at the nightclub, but so far, investigators have found no matching results.

While at The Thrill, Faith was reportedly dancing with a man named David Bell. He told police he didn't know Faith very well, and was not named by police as a suspect during the investigation.

"(Redacted) was identified as walking out of Club Thrill with Faith Hedgepeth shortly before the homicide occurred," read a police report unsealed in 2014. "He was the last male to be seen with her before her death."

The report added that Bell admitted to talking with Faith the night she was killed, and to meeting her the weekend before. He refused to provide investigators with a sample of his DNA, claiming that he had likely touched her at some point during the night of the homicide. His statements to law enforcement officers were also determined to be "inconsistent" with statements provided by others.

Another man, Jacob Beatley, was interviewed by police and also not named as a suspect. Karena visited him during the early morning hours of September 7, after leaving the apartment she shared with Faith. DNA was also sought from a man named Reginald Leonard Jackson II, who was not named as a suspect despite having been texting regularly with Faith in the days prior to her murder.

However, none of this information was offered to Faith's family until the documents were unsealed in 2014.

"All they have said to us and to the public, to the media, to everybody, (is) that this wasn't random – how do they know that?" said Chad Hedgepeth, Faith's brother. "Do they have a suspect? Do they have any suspects? ... Tell us something, because being in the dark on any and everything these past four weeks has been brutal."

While the recording from the 911 call seems to indicate that Karena was alone when she discovered Faith's body in their apartment, the police report stated that she returned to their home with a friend. In the recording, however, Karena consistently claims "I just walked into my apartment," instead of saying "we." There is also no sound recorded that could be attributed to another person in the room.

An analysis of the call could suggest that the repetition of the statement "I just walked into my apartment" is an attempt to establish an alibi – especially since the recording reveals that Karena says this several times before even providing the dispatcher with necessary information like the victim's state or the location of the emergency.

At no point in the call does Karena specifically ask for help for the victim. She also apologizes to the dispatcher, using language that analysts typically see in calls where guilty knowledge is indicated.

Initially, law enforcement turned their attention to Eriq Takoy Jones – an ex-boyfriend of Karena's who lived in the same apartment complex and was reportedly an aspiring rapper. Just a few months before the murder, Karena had filed a restraining order against Eriq, on the basis of domestic assault. Police had previously investigated claims that Eriq had kicked two of the doors in the girls' apartment completely off their frames, and eyewitness accounts reported that Karena had been seen with visible injuries to her body – inflicted, she said, by her ex-boyfriend.

"Faith took Karena to take out a restraining order," said Faith's father, Roland Hedgepeth. "I think that very possibly, Takoy may have had some ill feelings toward Faith for doing that."

Rolanda said Faith had moved in with Karena after the restraining order had been filed, to help her friend as she recovered from the abusive relationship.

"I wasn't worried about Faith at the time," Rolanda said. "I wanted them to be safe. I just wanted both of them to be safe."

Just before Faith was murdered, Eriq posted a chilling message on his Facebook page, and texted a similar message to an acquaintance.

"Deal Lord," the post read. "Forgive me for all of my sins and the sins I may commit today. Protect me from the girls who don't deserve me and the ones who wish me dead today."

An unnamed person who claimed to be a former roommate of Faith's called the Chapel Hill Police Department the day after Faith's body was discovered with additional concerning information about Eriq. According to the caller, Faith had told her that Karena's boyfriend hated her (Faith) and told her that if Karena wouldn't get back together with him, he would kill Faith.

However, Eriq was very cooperative with law enforcement during the investigation into Faith's murder. Both his apartment and car were combed for trace evidence, and his DNA was tested and cleared.

"From what I knew of her (Faith), she was the sweetest person in the world. If you needed her and she could do it, she was there," Eriq told news reporters after Faith's murder. "I'll be honest with you – whoever did this deserves to burn."

Investigators also learned that the ex-boyfriend of Karena's that Faith had texted in the hours before she was killed had also been present that night at The Thrill. Police records indicated that Brandon Edwards had even spent the night at the girls' apartment the night before the murder – making his response to Faith's texts the day she was killed quite unusual.

According to a friend named Marisol Rangel, Karena and Brandon were "just friends" at the time of Faith's murder. Marisol is the friend who was reportedly with Karena when she discovered Faith's body, but the 911 operator was confident that Karena was alone when the call was placed.

In January 2013, police released a profile of the killer. According to the profile, developed by Chapel Hill Police and the FBI's Behavioral Analysis Unit, the person responsible for Faith's murder might have been familiar with her – and possibly even lived near her in the past.

The individual may have also "made comments" about Faith in the past, with their behavior shifting after the murder occurred. Obviously, the profile indicated this person would have been "unaccounted for" during the early morning hours of September 7, 2012. Police also stated the DNA evidence collected at the scene of the homicide points toward a "male suspect."

At the time, Faith's father Roland said the development of the profile marked a "new beginning" in the investigation, and believed it would help police solve the case.

"For us, we're kind of stuck back on September 7," he said. "Every day, we get up and relive that day. But I'm confident things will open up soon."

Strange evidence

Nearly two years after the murder, police released a shocking and mysterious piece of evidence. A spiteful, handwritten note was found scrawled on a fast food bag left near the crime scene, with the words "I'M NOT STUPID BITCH JEALOUS."

Police believe the note was written by the killer, but have not said whether the handwriting has ever been officially analyzed. According to private investigator and forensic handwriting examiner Peggy Walla, some clues can be determined from the note.

"What struck me was how clean the document is – the crime scene was pretty bloody, and there's nothing on this document," she said. "Looking at it, I would get the impression it was either written outside of the crime scene, or it was written before, like a premeditation."

She also feels the words were written by a non-dominant hand, indicating that whoever wrote the note was attempting to "disguise" their penmanship. The block letters could be taken as the writer's attempt to distance themselves from authority, she said.

"The word and sentence phrase 'I'm not stupid' is a hot push-button factor," Walla added. "That's probably the most important thing said. This was a jealous person who was called 'stupid.' The person that said it who is now deceased has no way of repeating this person is stupid, which is another way to shut them up."

Users of online forums have also speculated that the use of the word 'jealous' could indicate that the writer of the note was a woman, as the word is thought to be more frequently used by females. The formation of the letter 'P' in particular has also struck some as seeming feminine in nature.

Other speculation surrounds the intent of the note. The words 'jealous' and 'bitch' suggest that the note was not meant for the police of for the public – rather, these deeply personal words were likely intended toward Faith, or possibly even Karena, who would eventually find the body. But more curious yet is the situation that must have occurred that led to the writing of the note. What happened before Faith was murdered?

Cries for help

A clue may be found in a voicemail left for a friend the night of her death. The call appears to have been a pocket-dial – a very timely pocket-dial that potentially recorded the final minutes of Faith's life. The timestamp on the nearly unintelligible message indicates that the call was made while Faith was still at The Thrill, but some have argued that a glitch in technology could have resulted in an incorrect time.

According to President and CEO of Creative Forensic Services Arlo West, who is certified by the New York Institute of Forensic Audio in enhancement, authentication, and analysis of both audio and video, the names 'Rosie' and 'Eriq' appear throughout the recording – potentially referring to Karena Rosario and her ex-boyfriend Eriq Takoy Jones.

"I've worked on hundreds, if not thousands, of cases where people have pocket-dialed somebody," West said. "If you can peel back those layers of noise, you start to get a better picture of the dialogue that is contained – stuff that starts to make a little more sense."

In his analysis for Crime Watch Daily, West identified two distinct female voices – one which he claimed is Faith Hedgepeth, and the other he describes as a "very angry female." He also picked out at least two male voices.

"I hear what I believe is Miss Hedgepeth's cries for help," West said. "You can hear her emotive voice, the tone of her voice, is clearly in pain … You can clearly hear what I believe is Faith pleading. She's being hurt, being attacked."

West said he feels "very confident" about hearing the names 'Rosie' and 'Eriq,' and included both names in his transcript of the three-minute recording.

He also claims iPhones were "inherently problematic with timestamping" during the time Faith was killed – which he said accounts for the timestamp on the voicemail showing 1:23 a.m., while police believe Faith was killed sometime after 4:30 a.m. Still, Chapel Hill police did contact West for an official analysis of the recording.

"If it is Faith being murdered, and captured in this recording – which I think it is, this is pivotal," West said. "It should be able to solve this case."

Police seem to believe that the voicemail was recorded from the club, not from the apartment – and in the middle of the call, there appears to be music playing or someone rapping. There is also no evidence to support that the name 'Rosie' could have referred to Karena, and Eriq Takoy Jones was apparently called 'Takoy' by his friends.

Still, the voicemail is difficult to discount – especially since, on the night Faith was murdered, it appears to have recorded an emotionally-charged, angry discussion. To many listeners, including members of Faith's family, the voices sound agitated – belligerent, fast-speaking – and seem to be punctuated by audible yelps of what could be pain.

"From day one, I heard my daughter screaming in the background," said Faith's father, Roland. "I knew something was going on."

"A really good case."

The note, the voicemail audio, and other documents – including the 15-page autopsy – were unsealed in September 2014. According to Chris Blue, Chapel Hill Police Chief, the effort was an attempt to generate new leads in the investigation.

"We have excellent evidence – we have a really good case," he said. "We just need to connect this really good case with the killer."

However, in those two years, police had been unable to connect any potential suspect with the crime. The official documents were sealed during that time despite repeated requests from lawyers and news organizations to open them to the public, as investigators felt releasing the information would compromise their efforts.

"It's not that it might hinder this investigation, it will hinder this investigation," said Durham County Assistant District Attorney Charlene Franks.

She added that details contained within the documents, including the 911 call where the crime scene and body are vividly described, could help police identify the killer – as that information would have been known by very few people.

In a "cold case," Franks said, police will often turn to the public for assistance. However, since the investigation into Faith's murder is ongoing, solving the case means keeping the public – including Faith's family – in the dark about some vital details.

"The most important thing to them and the state and the Chapel Hill Police Department is to find the killer of their baby girl, Faith Hedgepeth," she said. "The only way to do that is to keep those items sealed because the information contained in there, other than (investigators), only the killer knows."

According to Steve Hale, private investigator and retired homicide detective who was never involved with the case, it's typical for law enforcement to keep the details of a case under wraps – interviews and tips that haven't been influenced by media reports can make or break a case.

"If there is a suspect, he may not know he's a suspect, and they're waiting for him to get careless and maybe make a comment to an accessory after the fact," he said, adding that detectives likely suspected someone who knew Faith and might have had a distinct motive.

Each document pertaining to the case was reviewed by Judge Howard Manning before being unsealed in 2014. Still, three investigators with the Chapel Hill Police Department and State Bureau of Investigation continued working exclusively on the unsolved case – and offered a reward of $40,000 for any information leading to the arrest and conviction of Faith's killer.

"We really want to bring some peace to Faith's family," said Blue. "This has been two unimaginable years for them."

"Your imagination starts to run wild."

Connie was contacted three hours after Faith's body was found, by a crisis counselor who told her little more than that her 19-year-old daughter Faith had been found dead in her apartment – the victim of what appeared to be a violent homicide.

"I said, 'you must have the wrong girl,'" Connie remembers. "She told me it was her, and I said, 'I don't think so.'"

It fell on Connie to contact the rest of the family, spreading the devastating news to her son, her ex-husband, and her eldest daughter, Rolanda. At that point, Connie said, she didn't have much to tell them other than that Faith was dead.

"They couldn't tell us very much because they didn't want to jeopardize the investigation," she explained. "Not knowing anything at all... your imagination starts to run wild."

Even after detectives brought the family to Chapel Hill, about 80 miles away from their home in Hollister, Connie still had no answers to her many questions. She wasn't even permitted to visit the crime scene, or see her youngest daughter.

"I just wanted to hold her hand, to let her know I was there," Connie recalled. "I still cry for my baby, and I wonder if she called out for help. Did she cry for me? These are the things you think."

Finally, the family was told the cause of death – but without any kind of motive or indication of what could have happened to lead up to Faith's murder, the new information was difficult for the family to process.

"It is getting harder, not knowing what happened, trying to accept what happened," said Rolanda. "She was beautiful. She didn't deserve it. She had a lot going for her."

While no arrests have been made, and no suspects even identified, Chapel Hill Police Lt. Josh Mecimore said police are still confident that the killer will be found and brought to justice.

"Someone knows something, and we're continually appealing to the public to come forward," he said. "This is not a cold case. We are still following up on things, still pounding the pavement, still waiting for that one piece of evidence that will help us solve this case."

Connie, Rolanda, and the rest of the Hedgepeth family are clinging to the same hope.

"At some point, God will let us know what happened," Rolanda said. "Even when I'm down, I still believe that we will find that person."

However, neighbours remain concerned as a result of the limited information available – and the fact that police have yet to make an arrest. While law enforcement officers continued to reassure nearby residents that the incident was an isolated event, neighbours wanted more answers.

"It's not a reassuring thought to wonder if you can send your kids to safety to the bus stop or if something could happen," said Anna Salomon, who lived with her husband and children in the subdivision next to the apartment complex where Faith was murdered. In the weeks following the killing, the neighbours banded together to walk children to the bus stop in collective groups.

Keeping Faith alive

One year after Faith was killed, students at the University of North Carolina gathered on campus at the Bell Tower Amphitheatre for a silent walk in celebration of the student's life. She was also made an honorary member of the Alpha Pi Omega Sorority, the country's oldest Native American Greek letter organization.

"She was the happiest person I knew, always laughing, always smiling," said Faith's friend Leslie Locklear.

Another friend, Victoria Chavis, remembered Faith's "bubbly personality."

"She had a smile that was just infectious," she said, "and she was a wonderful person to be around."

"The entire Carolina community grieves for the loss of this promising, vibrant student," added UNC Chancellor Carol Folt.

The family has honored Faith's memory by establishing the "Faith's Smile Scholarship" in her name – an award which will go to Native American women entering their freshman year of college. The scholarship project gives the family something positive to focus on while they continue searching for answers.

"It's really hard – hard because of not knowing what happened and not knowing why it happened, who did it," Rolanda added. "One little piece of information could break the case, could give us some type of peace. How could somebody withhold that, after everything we have lost?"

Still, for Connie, nothing can extinguish the shining light that defined her youngest daughter, Faith – no matter how many years go by with the case remaining unsolved.

"We don't want anyone to forget her smile. She was a beautiful girl, she was my baby," Connie said. "Her spirit is right here today."

bonus:

On a seemingly normal Thursday afternoon on the Catawba River in May of 2008, two jet skiers planned on having a picnic together along the river when they stumbled upon a peculiar sight that would change their lives forever - a car crashed into a stump on the banks of the river along with the horrifying sight of a dead body lying next to it. They quickly alerted authorities and soon discovered that the body was that of a deceased young woman.

This was the tragic fate of Irina "Ira" Yarmolenko, a University of North Carolina college student who had just celebrated her twentieth birthday several days earlier. She was discovered with three items from her car tied around her neck. There was no sign of a struggle or any clear indication of a motive. She was not sexually assaulted or robbed.

Although first responders initially thought her death could have been a suicide, her death was ruled a homicide by asphyxiation. To this day, her murder still garners interest from the public due to the strange yet disturbing circumstances surrounding her death. Add to that the whispers that surround the case about the possibility that her convicted murderer, Mark Carver, might actually be an innocent man. What followed this horrific discovery was an investigation into the crime scene and into her personal life to uncover what happened to Ira.

Ira's early life and college experience

Ira Yarmolenko was born in the Ukraine on May 2nd, 1988 but emigrated to the United States when she was eight, along with her parents and brother Pavel. The family reportedly fled the Ukraine as refugees due to religious persecution. Her parents, both research scientists, were able to find job opportunities in North Carolina.

Ira quickly picked up the language and by all accounts seemed to assimilate well into American culture. She lived in North Carolina for most of her life, spoke with a southern accent and had several personal interests. Like most teenagers, she enjoyed hiking, acting, photography, sports, and music.

She also played the piano and liked listening to bands, such as the Counting Crows. She was also extremely academic. She excelled in math and science while being an active member of her high school poetry team. Ira was especially close to her family. Although she left Chapel Hill for UNC Charlotte, about a 3-hour drive away, she spoke to her mother almost every day. After her death, her mother said to reporters, "I don't think what I'm living is called life anymore."

During her two years in college, she found other interests beyond her required coursework at UNC Charlotte, where she was an undeclared major but had a strong interest in French. She was a photographer for the University Times, her college paper, and occasionally wrote columns and articles for the Niner Online, an online student-run newspaper.

She was also a member of the university's Russian Club as Russian was her first language. Her Russian language classmate described her as, "the kind of girl that always made you feel special, wanted, needed, cared for, and loved. It always seemed like she was always so happy to see you, and would always take at least a second of her time to say hello to you." It was here that she met her roommate Masha, another student from the Ukraine.

Masha and Ira bonded over the fact that they both spoke Russian and came from similar backgrounds. Masha described the day that she found out Ira was murdered when two investigators showed up at the small apartment that she shared with Ira, "It was her student I.D. picture. And I just started screaming. Sorry. Both of our families immigrated here to this country for a better life and sacrificed so much." Like most people close to Ira, Masha was devastated to hear the news of her friend's death.

Most people who knew Ira described her as outgoing. They felt that she would not have been afraid if a stranger had approached her. She was involved on campus and worked at a local coffee shop, Jackson's Java. Years after her death, her picture could still be found on the counter of Jackson's Java. She had a lasting impact on those that knew her. Her brother said, "Everything that she's ever done was to help people."

At UNC Charlotte, she had many close friends and acquaintances who described her as a cheerful and bubbly person, yet still high-achieving. In addition to her job at the coffee shop, Ira also worked as an aid in a computer lab on campus. The week before finals, her roommate Masha and friends threw a party for her 20th birthday.

During this party, her friends reported that Ira ended up cooking for everyone there, despite the fact that party was a celebration in her honor. This was not uncommon for her to do and was just the kind of person she was. Her friends concluded the celebration by visiting an art exhibit. They reported that she was in good spirits and that they parted amicably.

Although it seemed Ira was thriving in her environment at UNC Charlotte, she was in the process of closing her chapter there and beginning a new one at UNC-Chapel Hill, a school a bit closer to home. "Ira indicated she was sad to leave her friends behind at UNCC, but she was looking forward to attending UNC-Chapel Hill in the fall," according to Sgt. Tindall, an investigator in the case.

She had resigned from her positions at the coffee shop and in the computer lab where she had worked during her sophomore year shortly before she was murdered. Her brother Pavel, a then Ph.D. graduate student at Duke said, "She was not sure how she felt about leaving Charlotte. But she was very, very excited about coming to Chapel Hill."

Ira intended on transferring to UNC-Chapel Hill to be closer to her family and to major in public health. The day of her murder, she visited the coffee shop and said goodbye to her friends there and left a gift, a book, for her former boss. She also took several items to the Goodwill to donate and visited her credit union where she deposited some checks before heading to the river about 20 miles away.

The scene of the crime

The Catawba River is over 200 miles long and spans two states. It is located about 20 minutes from Charlotte and is popular among fisherman, boaters and jet skiers. First responders on that fateful day described a perplexing, yet disturbing scene.

The doors on the driver's side of Ira's car were opened, and her body was found just a few feet away. It did not appear she was sexually assaulted or robbed, nor did she have defensive wounds from fighting off her attacker or attackers.

Three ligatures were found around her neck: a nylon ribbon from a bag in her car, a drawstring from the hood of a jacket and a bungee cord. The drawstring was wrapped around her neck. The ribbon was wrapped once around her neck and oddly tied in a bow in the front. Her hair and body were also wet, although she was found on dry ground.

According to Detective Terry during the trial, "Her head was back towards the embankment. Her feet were near the river underneath some brush. Upon closer inspection, she was actually holding some of that brush in her hand. . . ." It was determined that this was the place where she was murdered and that she had not been transferred there.

Investigators began piecing together her movements before arriving at the river banks and determined it was likely that she headed down to the river banks to take pictures, as she was an avid photographer. Her brother Pavel said he "wasn't surprised she would go to such a remote spot. She was adventurous. She once hiked the Stampede Trail in Alaska with friends, searching for an abandoned bus made famous by Jon Krakauer's book Into the Wild."

Her camera was found in the trunk of her car, but there was not any film in it that could yield any clues about her death. Investigators quickly began interviewing people along the river to see if anyone had heard or seen anything out of the ordinary and came across two fishermen who were fishing about 100 yards from where Ira's body and car were discovered.

Mark Carver and Neil Cassada were cousins who grew up in the area and had been fishing in a new spot they had discovered the weekend before. This spot was about 100 yards from where Ira's car and body were discovered. Carver had been excited about the spot. He had returned to it because it did not require him to haul his boat to the river which was difficult for Carver to do since he suffers from carpal tunnel syndrome, a condition that makes his hands extremely weak.

His doctors recommended he not lift anything heavier than five pounds. Cassada also suffered from a heart condition, making it difficult to do anything too physical. Investigators questioned both men who reported that they had not seen Ira or had not heard anything from their fishing spot. They did report hearing a scraping sound that sounded like noise from construction.

They both willingly provided their DNA to investigators and went on their way. With the lack of forensic clues pointing toward any viable suspects, it was not until forensic analysis of the car several months later revealed partial DNA matches for Carver and Cassada that they became the prime suspects for Ira's murder. Mark Carver and Neal Cassada were arrested in December of 2008, seven months after her death and charged with conspiracy and murder. A day before Cassada's the trial began in 2010, Cassada died of a heart attack. Carver has always proclaimed their innocence.

"Simple" life of Mark Carver

Simple is the word often used to describe Mark Carver. "Simple in his routine, simple in his thought process, simple in his desires and wants," defense attorney Brent Ratchford said to reporters. Unlike Ira, Carver is not well-educated and has limitations with writing and reading comprehension, which he has struggled with throughout most of his life.

At an early age, he was placed in special education classes because of these limitations and his relatively low IQ. At 16, he dropped out of school to work in a mill. At the time he was arrested, it was documented that he was taking medication prescribed for schizophrenia.

Carver is also the father of four children from two different marriages. "He lived for his children and family," his sister-in-law Robin Carver said when asked about him. "He didn't really do much of anything else. Fishing and hunting and family, that was about it."

Although his family speaks well of Carver, like most family members often do, he did have prior brushes with the law despite never being convicted of a crime. In 2005, Carver faced a charge of injury to property. Carver purportedly confronted two people he thought were stealing his four-wheeler. The charge was dismissed, and the file no longer exists. A year before Ira's murder, Carver accidentally shot his son. Carver and his son were supposedly wrestling when the gun went off. "It was an accident," his son said. The case was later dismissed and Carver never convicted of a crime.

Cassada also had had his own dealings with the law. In 1995, he was accused of assault and injury to personal property. He reportedly pointed a gun at someone. But the charges were dismissed and the details remain unclear.

His family insists that he had nothing to do with Ira's murder and that the stress of the trial for a crime he did not commit ultimately led to his death. Kaye Cassada, Neal Cassada's wife said "After 37 years of loving that man and being married to that man, I know he is not capable of hurting anybody. He would have died to help somebody." Charges against Cassada were dropped, a common proceeding with deceased suspects. His family attended the hearing and his son Shannon Cassada said, "We want everybody to hear that he was an innocent man."

Carver also maintains his own innocence, stating "they said that they had ... my DNA and Neal's DNA in the car. I know that's a lie because Neal left, and they couldn't have gotten no DNA because I wasn't down there. I didn't go around it. I didn't go around the car. You know what I'm saying?" He also said he didn't think Cassada would commit such a crime because "He's got four young'uns himself."

Although lie detector tests are not reliable enough to be used in court, during the initial investigation Cassada took a polygraph test, which he passed. Because he passed, investigators did not give Carver one. Carver has been very vocal about his willingness to also take a polygraph test.

Touch DNA

During the investigation and trial, Carver never wavered in proclaiming his innocence and said this to Ira's family "I never seen her that day. If I'd knowed she was up there, I would have went up there and helped her. They could have easily come down and killed me just like they did her."

His trial began in 2010. Before the trial, Carver was offered a surprising plea deal from the prosecution: 4-8 years in prison if he pleaded guilty to second degree murder. Had he taken this deal and pled guilty to murder he could be out of prison and with his family. His attorney said, "I have never gotten such a low offer. And to me that spoke volumes about the case." Carver turned down this offer and prosecutors moved forward with the case.

Prosecutors argued that the two men killed Ira because she witnessed or photographed something they did not want her to see. As a result, they strangled her and pushed her car on the embankment where their DNA was transferred to the car. Their intention was to sink the car in the water, but it hit a stump where it stayed until it was finally discovered by the jet skiers. They then returned to their fishing spot until they were questioned by police.

Prosecutors relied on a relatively new forensic technique at the time known as "touch DNA." Unlike previous methods, touch DNA uses smaller amounts of DNA, such as skin cells transferred to a person or object when they come into contact with someone. But touch DNA is not as reliable as other DNA methods requiring blood or saliva because it is difficult to determine the origin of these cells. For instance, skin cells can be transferred indirectly by a third party or carrier.

For example, a man in California was falsely imprisoned because his DNA was found on a murder victim. It was determined that it was impossible that he was a killer because he had a solid alibi. At the time of the murder, he was unconscious in a hospital due to extreme intoxication.

Prosecutors then discovered that the same paramedic who treated him for intoxication was a first responder at the murder scene. The DNA from the intoxicated man was presumably transferred to the victim by the paramedic. This case set a precedent about the reliability of touch DNA and is cited by Carver's advocates for innocence as a possibility as to why Carver's and Cassada's DNA was found on Ira's car.

Despite this interesting theory, it was not presented by the defense in Carver's trial and the jury found him guilty of murder. He was sentenced to and is currently serving life in prison. Carver's advocates argue that the car and crime scene was not preserved, and that Carver and Cassada's DNA could have been transferred by officers or other people near the crime scene. Many officers, the jet skiers, first responders were all present at the crime scene and could have all inadvertently transferred the DNA to the car.

Several other inconsistencies exist in the prosecution's case. Carvers DNA was not found on her body nor on the trunk of the car where he and Cassada would have pushed it into the river bank according to prosecutors. Carvers DNA did not match a third DNA profile found on the bungee cord and the only DNA found under Ira's fingernails was her own.

His attorney and advocates also argue that the two men couldn't have physically pushed the car into the river bank due to Carver's carpal tunnel and Cassada's heart condition. Cassada supposedly got winded just walking. In 2013, Carver's attorneys filed an appeal on his behalf, but the appeals court determined "no error in the defendant's trial" occurred, meaning his conviction of life in prison would be upheld. But this did not deter his advocates from trying to prove Carver did not receive a fair defense during his trial.

Earlier this year, a judge granted the request of the North Carolina Actual Innocence Project, attorneys who have become interested in Carver case who believe Carver is wrongfully imprisoned, to see DNA reports that were never shared with Carvers defense team, along with further DNA testing.

They argue that Carver did not receive a proper defense as his lawyers did not call any witnesses or DNA experts to the stand and address the DNA evidence, and that the DNA evidence is not compelling enough beyond a reasonable doubt to warrant a life sentence for Carver. It is the only evidence linking Carver to the crime. Only time will determine the final outcomes of Carver's appeals as the evidentiary hearing has been postponed. Legal proceedings could take several years.

Other suspects

If Carver and Cassada's DNA was indeed transferred by a third party and they did not kill Ira, then who did? There was no one in her life that seemed to have any motive. Besides these two men, there was only one other suspect in her murder investigation. Nine months after the murder, Christopher Lemont Cooper wrote a letter to News anchor Erica Bryant to "confess a sin," that he and several other accomplices had killed Ira.

He said he drove a van full of friends that were all high and needed money for drugs. He said he was unable to sleep "because of what we did to that young woman." And wished to meet with the reporter. The TV station did not publish the letter and turned it over to investigators where they took the letter very seriously and launched an investigation with the North Carolina State Bureau of Investigations.

Police and investigators visited Cooper, where he was in jail on charges of rape, assault by strangulation, and for being delinquent in child support. He reportedly refused to cooperate with investigators, but they ultimately ruled him out as a suspect concluding that several of the accomplices he named were incarcerated at the time of the murder. They also cleared the other accomplices named in Cooper's letter and continued building their case against Carver and Cassada.

Free Mark Carver

Free Mark Carver is one of the prominent websites advocating for the release of Carver. They believe he is innocent or at the very least did not receive a proper defense in his trial. The website is run by a former newspaper journalist who now works in the fashion industry. She had no ties to the case or families and became intrigued with the case in 2011 after its details aired on Dateline NBC and through other online news articles.

One of the major theories from Carver's advocates presented on the website is that Ira was not murdered and in fact committed suicide by placing the ligatures around her neck herself. They claim that Ira was not the cheerful person described by her friends and loved ones and that she had battled depression.

Her boyfriend had broken up with her shortly before her murder and her poetry was sometimes dark and melancholy. The website alludes to accounts from unnamed people who claim that Ira had attempted suicide when she was younger and had seen a therapist at UNC Charlotte. The website does not provide sources and only mentions them as letters to the author.

Although this theory may be offensive to those who loved Ira and describe her as a happy and vibrant young woman, it has been addressed by pathologists who have dismissed this theory saying "For this to have been anything but a homicide, i.e., this was a suicide, this victim would have to tie three ligatures around her neck tightly and before death get into this position while that's going on and her legs underneath the brush given that position and I just feel like that was not consistent with what we are seeing. . . . Yes, and another thing that this illustrates a little bit better also is the presence of particular matter, soil and grass on her skirt as well. So that's another thing that would have had to happen. If this was a suicide she would have had to do all this stuff by herself. It is just not consistent with that theory."

Her brother Pavel, who has since completed his Ph.D. in biomedical engineering and continues to conduct research at a pediatric hospital, said he has read some of the internet theories about his sister's death, but they are "not grounded in reality." He asserts that his sister never attempted suicide and there was no indication she was depressed. Nevertheless, the fact remains that a lively, young woman lost her life just days after her 20th birthday.

Memorials

We may never know what really happened to Ira or why someone chose to take her life but it is clear that she touched many people who strive to keep her memory alive. The jet skiers who found her body, Dennis Lovelace and Brenda Pierce, placed a memorial cross where they found her car. The changing levels of the Catawba river sometimes covers part of the cross, but it is still visible to visitors.

A memorial bench as far as Alaska, where Ira spent a summer waitressing, also bears her name. "A Kansas City based artist Shane Blindt designed and installed this bench at the request of many co-workers whose lives were touched with Ira's presence during the 2007 McKinley Village Lodge summer season. Lettering on the memorial was hand drawn with pen showing the elegance and beauty of Ira's outward expressions contrasted with a raw and rugged placement into the world she left behind." It is maintained by locals there.

Her high school poetry team in Chapel Hill renamed the group The Sacrificial Poets in her honor.

What Time Devours is a book written by her former professor at UNC Charlotte who dedicated his book to her memory. He directed a campus production, which Ira was a part of the previous year before she was murdered. He also included a line from her poetry and her picture in the dedication of the book.

The controversy around her murder continues to intrigue people and several websites and pages are dedicated to outlining the details of the case. Ira's murder has been featured on Dateline and 20/20. She continues to captivate an almost cult following, and many people are still tirelessly working to prove that Carver is innocent and did not receive a fair trial. If this is the case, it means that justice has not been served for Ira and her family. But one thing is for sure, the memory of Ira Yarmolenko will continue to live on with her family, friends, and strangers that have been touched by her story.